REINVENT YOURSELF

Achieving the Impossible Using Science

Elizabeth Otis

Reinvent Yourself

All references and quotations are listed in the back of the book.

Published in the United States of America

Copyright © 2020 Elizabeth Otis

Request for information should be directed to the contact page of the Publishing Company's website. All rights reserved. No part of this publication may be reproduced, stored in a retrieval system, or transmitted in any form of by any means- electronic, mechanical, recording, or any other – except for brief quotations in printed reviews, without the prior permission of the publisher.

Table of Contents

Intro: There's a Science from Point A to Z   5

Chapter 1: Know Your True Magic   12

Chapter 2: It's Been Screaming for You   25

Chapter 3: You Literally Had No Idea   37

Chapter 4: It's All About Matching   47

Chapter 5: Who's the Captain in Control?   64

Chapter 6: This is Your Best Friend   109

Chapter 7: Logically It Doesn't Make Sense   122

Chapter 8: Imagine A World Where   129

Chapter 9: You Are Legendary   135

Introduction – There's a Science From Point A to Z

If you KNEW you could achieve whatever you wanted, is it possible to feel any sort of doubt? Do you think you would operate out of fear? Do you think you'd ever play small? Be stopped from going after what you *truly* wanted??... ABSOLUTELY NOT!

So why is it that we would ever do such a thing? You're right! You even said it yourself: It's because of our conditioning. We don't *fully* believe that we can achieve and be whatever we wanted to otherwise we would be doing & being it. At least, we don't believe this without having to add some amount of pain to our lives that wouldn't outweigh the pleasure of obtainment.

Although I'd like to inspire you as much as possible, this book isn't just to inspire you to think in a bigger way and encourage you to go for it. What I'm here to do is teach you how to apply, step by step, the science behind any obtainment so that you can experience the life you've always envisioned for yourself. Yes, you read that right. Everything in this universe has an equation.

You see, you can have BOTH. You can have it all, *really*. It's not a question of whether you'd rather do this or that, have this or that. It's the question of, "how can I give myself the experience of having all that I truly desire?"

Through the science explained in this book, you will gain clarity on how to physically experience what you desire and live out your purpose. Universal laws have proved to us that everything is made up of the same energy. Everything is the same, just in different expressions of its *original* form. Science has proved to us that everything has a vibration, & when you match something vibrationally, it is what you experience likewise in your outer reality. The deeper question is then, "how do I embrace all that I truly desire that is within me?"

The purpose behind this book is very clear. It's

to show you how to experience a new reality for yourself. Not a reality that you'd be just *satisfied* with... I'm talking about the kind of reality that allows you to fulfill your purpose, experience your wildest desires, do what you feel called for, and most importantly, be *truly* YOU.

There are infinite realities all going on at once that are avalible to you. What determines what you are experiencing is what you are aligning with vibrationally... what frequency your vibration is resonating at. Just like in order for a radio station to receive sound, we have to first be in the receptive frequency. We have to be in the frequency of that which we desire in order to ever obtain it.

It doesn't matter who you know, how hard you work, or what strategy you have if your energy, your vibrational frequency, is out of alignment with that which you want. All of those things are important but, you will mess those things up for yourself and **literally** be physically be blind/deaf to opportunities right in front of you if you are out of alignment with those desires. That's why people could be doing all the right "things" in order to get them from point A to Z but never accomplish it despite everything they did in order to receive or experience it.

As we dive further into this book, I have to give a warning for this book will challenge your belief system, introduce resistance, & potentially trigger some emotional disturbance. The reason being is, you will literally be reprogramming yourself, *changing your DNA*. Healing is going to take place. Your current reality, for what you know it as, WILL be shifted. You'll discover hidden "truths" you have inside of you that have been putting blocks up in your life. However, there is nothing to fear because it is all for your benefit. What you are really doing is unmasking all the junk in front of everything that is truly you. Picture it like this, you are a pure, bright, infinite light….simply energy. The **same energy** that creates worlds but, has its own, unique purpose for creation; unique purpose of being. Anything "blocking" this light from being, doing, and experiencing all it's pure desires is it's shadow. You're bringing your shadow to the light in order to experience the vibrational transformation that aligns you to the frequency of that which you truly desire.

We all came here for a purpose and the time has come for you to experience it. I'm not saying that to just pump your head up either. That is something that has been scientifically proven which we will be addressing in depth further in the book.

So, before we go any further, it's important to keep an open mind if you are ready to start seeing the results you want to have in your life & feel true, deep satisfaction. Like I said, resistance will be brought up & when it does, it's critical that it be worked through with the tools you are given because it's this exact way of thinking, being, *vibrating*, that causes you to not experience what you want.

You always hear the phrases: "it takes time","practice makes perfect","work hard","give more value" when it comes to succeeding and phrases like "just love yourself the way you are","just be grateful for what you have" when it comes to wanting to improve ourselves and the way we feel. Although they are all good pieces of advice, alone, or even all together, they aren't what's going to give you the substantial results you want **_without_** the missing key discussed in this book.

Let's be real... If you are unsatisfied with yourself or with the results you have in your life, then something needs to change. There is NO reason why you should continuously live in a state of being anything less than joyous, at peace, infatuated for the majority of your waking moments. Yes, there will be moments of contrast to show us what we don't want in life, to guide us, to signal to us that we don't understand something, but, that's all it is. Emotions are signals. Whenever we are in alignment with our pure, infinite self, we feel states like joy, peace, love because this is our true, natural state of being. So, when we feel anything less than that, we can use our consciousness to remove the shadow triggering the low emotion and shift us to the reality we would like to experience.

You owe it to yourself to live out what you came here for & to feel charged, excited about life. You're on that path by reading this book. The big domino, the one that comes knocking down everything else needed, is the one that we are going to be addressing in this book. So without further-ado, let's dive in my friend.

Chapter 1 – Know Your True Magic

As we start to discuss how to be, feel and experience that which you want, you of course want to be clear on what that really is for you. It's critical that *that* is what it *actually is.* Meaning, it's coming from a place of authenticity, not in influence or directed by any sort of limitation. You can take the same fundamentals from this book, apply it to any desire, and get results. In order to have those results substantially, however, it has to be something that truly fulfills you. If you apply this knowledge based off of ego, to be accepted, what other people want for you, or because it's what you believe is more likely vs what you really want, not only will you not even care when you achieved it because you're not happy but, you'll also end up subconsciously self sabotaging yourself to the point where it unravels eventually anyway... leaving all your efforts to be crumbled once again.

Preparatory to getting "clear" on how you want to be, feel, and experience, it's also critical that you have locked in the belief that all things are achievable & that you have the ability to make so happen under universal laws. If this belief is not locked in, you are more than likely to limit yourself in what you have available to you.

For most people picking up this book, that idea seems far-fetched and you're going to need more proof to believe so. Raw spiritual based practices, as early as we know it, have been telling us this same information - just in different context. If you aren't already a spiritual person, however, you likely do not believe this without some sort of proof and I don't blame you. So, what we are going to start off discussing is how that exact same statement is now proven through science. In doing so, you will become certain that this is true. Once you are certain of this belief, you will then be taught on how to apply it so that you experience what you truly desire. - not a desire with limitations on it.

Diving in, I am now going to briefly explain some of our universal laws, human science, & how they play together in directly impacting our human experience above and before *anything* else.

Law of Oneness-

As stated in the introduction, the Law of Oneness teaches us that all energy comes from the same source. Energy IS… it cannot be created or destroyed. Everything is the same just in different expressions of each other. Everything *already* exists.

This means that you & I are made up of the same energy that created this entire world. It also means you are made from the same energy of the money you desire, the love you want to feel, the help you want to give. You are a part of the same energy that stardust and lightning comes from!

Law of Vibration-

This teaches us that everything in this universe is on a vibrational wavelength.

Nothing is still.

This even counts for non-physical matters such as thoughts, emotions, & forcefields. Our personal vibration is what energetic frequency our mental, emotional, physical bodies are resonating at. Which we will talk more about later.

Law of Attraction-

(as I'm sure you've now heard of) teaches us that whatever vibration we are carrying, we attract likewise into our experience.

We will explain why negative things happen even when you've been doing everything right later to clear up why negative events have happened in your life & why some people claim the Law of Attraction doesn't "work."

The Law of Perpetual Transmutation of Energy-

This law teaches us that all energy is not only vibrating and moving, but it's in a constant

state of transmutation. Energy that you can't even see is transmuting into each other right in front of you and through you. This is the law that allows our thoughts to become physical things. This is the law that states all energy from its original form can transmute into something else.

From this statement alone, you can now start to realize that "crazy or impossible" things like shapeshifting, is actually not so crazy and impossible afterall. It's actually possible, most people just haven't figured out how to do it yet. This law confirms that your dreams aren't so crazy or impossible after all... if you can think it, you can do it!

One thing to also to take note is consuming food/substances and being in a particular environment for the energy of those things transmute through you. We will talk more on how to leverage this and also how to protect yourself from it.

The last, FOR NOW, is the Law of Correspondence-

This law teaches us that our outer reality is a mirror of our inner reality. It states that there are multiple realities happening at this very moment & whatever we match internally, we experience externally. It also states that nothing happens at random, it's all for a reason. Everything you experience is relevant to you. This is the law that hammers in why we must align with the frequency we want first, just like a radio station.

With this being said, we will now expunge the idea of linear time. (meaning time happens with a past, present, and future). In the paragraph below, I explain what science has now proved to us about time so that you can really open yourself to the infinite possibilities of this universe. Most people think in an extremely limited way due to being conditioned with the perspective of linear time.

If you're anything like me, or used to be I should say, the whole idea that time doesn't have a past, present and future wouldn't sit right with me because how would you then explain things like aging &

development, right? So don't worry, I will explain how and why things like that take place in a linear-based perspective later in this book. For now, I am going to explain the difference between linear time (the old way of viewing time) and what we have now proved about time (simultaneous or quantum.)

Linear Time

PAST   PRESENT   FUTURE

Quantum Time

"Time" as we know it, is actually just an illusion and will leave you completely limited if you view it in a linear way. There is no past, present, or future. The only time is now. From the above images, you can see that the picture demonstrating simultaneous (quantum) time is a circle, with an arrow that says "time space reality you are experiencing" pointing in the circle at the word now. This is because it has been discovered that, relating to the Law of Correspondence, infinite realities are available in every moment and we are shifting in and out of them as we speak. Whatever you are perceiving is whatever your vibration is accustomed to, whatever frequency you are aligning with energetically. (note that energy doesn't just go in a counterclockwise motion but also, clockwise and vertical swirls.)

An example explaining this further can be pulled from Deepak Chopra, M.D.'s book, "Quantum Healing." In it he says: "... a single photon, electron, or any other object in the quantum world can never be seen using any extension of sight and touch. They are truly everywhere and nowhere at the same time."

To take this even further, Neuroscientist, Scott Grafton says that in order for anything to be real to our bodies, neurologically, there has to be some sort of "space" between it and your senses.

Time is a perception based upon how much space you put between what you currently are picking up with your senses and then comprehending what that means to you. Every experience you have in your life is due to the frequency you are in alignment with. What you believe is possible, how long it would take, what you feel worthy of and so forth.

Everything in this universe is already created. Everything is energy & energy is. What you want is already done & created. We are the ones who get to transmute this infinite energy into what we desire.

Since you now know everything is done and created, it's time to also know that you can be physically blind and deaf to real things happening right in front of you if you aren't reasoning with that frequency. We will be discussing later exactly why this is and how to target in on exactly what you prefer.

Put together simply with what you had learned earlier- Everything in the world already exists and whatever you receive and perceive in your human experience, is due to what you are aligning with mentally, physically, emotionally… what frequency your vibration is at.

An exciting, real world life example of this explanation would be winning the lottery. Linear time would say that in order to win the lottery, you must buy the correct ticket. You have to play a certain number, at a certain time, before somebody else beats you to it. Simultaneous time would state that in order to win the lottery, you buy *whatever* ticket, and *shift* to the reality of the winning ticket then scratch it off while you're in that frequency in order to win. Another example would be somebody just giving you a winning lottery ticket because you are in that frequency of receiving it. Since all things are possible for you at the same time, it's a matter of parallelly matching that "time" in space.

      Thinking from a linear time perspective leaves us extremely limited because experiencing the result you want never happens because you took this action, which lead to this action, which lead to this result or desired outcome. We always experience that which we are attracting to us through the vibrational frequency we are personally resonating with. It actually DOESN'T MATTER what you do as long as you hold the vibration of that which you want because of how energy actually works. There are no laws of the universe stating that you have to work x amount of hours to get this amount of pay, or call this many people to get something done, or do this many sit-ups to get the abs you want..... that is all an illusioned state of mind which then shapes our vibration to where WE HAVE to do those things in order to get those results because that's what we believe it takes to have it.

Picture it like this; you have an extremely powerful, magnetic ball in the core of your being that is drawing in absolutely everything it energetically resonates with. No matter what you are doing, whether that be hammering away at work, studying, swimming at the beach or laying in a hammock... whatever vibration that magnetic ball holds and is on the frequency of, it will attract to it and bring it into your experience. This is why opportunities seem to pop up out of nowhere and come straight to you when you feel like you don't need them anymore...Since the vibration of that magnetic ball shifted to the frequency of having, it effortlessly brought to your doorstep the energy you were already giving off. We want to start getting in the habit of already knowing, believing, that we are on the journey of experiencing that which we want. That we will obtain what that is no matter what so we are just enjoying the ride. When we come from this frame of mind, state of being, we shift our internal vibration to link the frequency of that which we want and are guided through many avenues of having that experience. You're never going to not experience that which you want from the action you didn't take; you'll only never experience it as long as your vibrational frequency is off from it because it magnetically can't come into your experience. That right there is the biggest paradigm shift for almost anybody reading this book because all of our lives we have grown up to believe energy works in a linear way... leaving us obsessed on constantly staying busy trying to get stuff done and adjusting our strategy when that's not the real work that needs to take place.

    As you know from what we just talked about, linear time is the old way of understanding how time works. Yet, it is what is still largely incorporated by our everyday lives through things like schedules, language, and thoughts. Because of that, throughout this book you will learn how to shift and operate in the quantum way of thinking even though the majority of the world is still thinking from a linear view.

RECAP!

Now I know that was a lot to take in and maybe it all didn't register as it truly is. So, I will give an overview of everything just said in order to anchor down the belief that all things are achievable under universal laws. That you can truly have it all. You can "reinvent" yourself to experience the reality you'd like to experience!

Science has now proved to us that everything already exists and that there are multiple realities in any given moment. All things are possible because everything is energy & energy is in a constant state of transmutation that has the ability to transmute into anything. We experience the reality that we desire whenever we internally match it. The frequency of our personal vibration is what determines what we give off internally.

Just like a radio station receiving messages, you first have to be in the frequency of that which you desire because it is only then that you can carry out the right thoughts, words, and actions to get you the results you want. It is only then that you will also be physically aware of it with your eyes, ears, and bodily senses. Having the right strategy, working harder, or connecting with more people will never get you what you want to experience if you're out of alignment with it. It's scientifically impossible yet, we are bombarded with messages and advertisements left and right telling us to work harder, try this new strategy out, get new leads this way, and so forth. If we are not getting the results we want, we must first ALWAYS look within.

So now that you are starting to embrace the infinite possibilities to you and acknowledging the personal power that you truly have, it's time to start transmuting that vibrational energy into physical energy so you can experience it in your physical reality. This next chapter is all about focusing on what it is you truly want. It's purpose is to identify what your pure, limitless desires are and to make sure that you don't believe in anything less for yourself.

Are you ready?

P.S. If you do not understand this chapter, **DO NOT**

go on to read any further until you really grasp what this all means. If this is the case, go back and read again. You can also connect and discuss these teachings with like-minded people in the BLIVE community to have a better understanding. It's crucial that you understand this first because if otherwise, your misunderstanding will bleed into your results and limit you. The link to the community is listed below for easy access.

www.facebook.com/groups/blivemovement

Chapter 2 –
It's Been Screaming For You

If you understood the first chapter and didn't skip ahead without doing so, I know you are absolutely fired up about what's available to you. Simultaneously, it's understandable that there's still some doubt wrapped around this concept personally. You may now have started to grasp the belief that what you TRULY want is achievable BUT... exactly that, there is BUT involved. Whether that be doubt based upon likelihood, if you're good enough, the list goes on.

It's understandable that you feel this way because you've had all this evidence slap you in the face that says so. Because of that, it was important for me to let you know that whenever you begin to start to have those feelings of doubt, relate it to the fact that it's like you are questioning the fact if 3+3=6 or not. You can relate it to this statement because what we're are talking about here is an equation. We will address how to eliminate all feelings of doubt in detail further on in this book so, for now, remember that simple statement. If we let feelings of uncertainty affect how we are feeling right now, that doubtful energy will transmute into the intentions we are putting out for ourselves during this next lesson.

This chapter is all about setting ***thee*** intentions you plan on experiencing due to applying what you learned in this book. This is where your heart and soul speaks. Like I said in the previous chapter, you can take the formula from this book, apply it to anything, and get results. We are looking ONLY to apply it to what is authentic to us however. Stepping into who we TRULY are. Even though this book is called "Reinvent Yourself," as stated in the introduction, what you are really doing is removing any limitations and influence on who you truly are. Do not be afraid to step into who that really is. The only reason why anybody would ever want to be anything other than who they truly are, is because they haven't taken inventory, have acknowledged and embraced, all of the unique, priceless value & beauty that only THEY bring to this world. Remember, I don't say this just to blow your head up. It's literal science that everybody has their own unique vibration and that nothing in this universe happens by accident. EVERYTHING HAPPENS FOR A REASON.

That being said, own who you are! You are more than amazing, you are the freaking energy that creates worlds. You are magnificent, you are priceless! Your pure desires have a reason behind them that benefit the planet as a whole. We are all connected. It's time to now set the intentions on what that aligns with. Those desires hold a strong place in this world. Let's put them to life.

First, we want to start with what you believe to be your purpose & how you want to be living your overall day to day life. It doesn't matter if you're reading this to amp up your love life, increase your financial status, make a massive impact in the world, or even change the way you look. If you design your life based upon anything other than how you authentically want to be living, you will not hit the level of fulfillment you want to feel. Remember, you can have it all. Don't set intentions to do something because it logically makes sense to achieve. Set intentions that align with the life you'd be living if it was all designed by you. - because it is. Now, if you haven't already identified your purpose, don't worry, it's simple using the below 3 steps:

#1 - Early Days
#2 - Flow
#3 - Eliminating Beliefs Around It

A big reason why most people don't end up fulfilling their purpose or are living a life they truly desire is because they get caught up believing that they have to take a particular pathway to fulfill their dreams vs identifying the fundamentals in what they love doing and living through them.

Let's use an example of teaching. A child begins to develop the interest and desire towards teaching but then get conflicted about pursuing it as they grow older because they think they would have to work in a school to achieve that or that they wouldn't get paid as much as they'd like. They get conflicted about pursuing it because simultaneously they want to live remote and be paid more than the average school teacher. It's conflicting beliefs like these that hold people back from even identifying what their true purpose even is initially and then simply not living out a life experience that fulfills them.

The thing is, there are infinite ways for you to express your purpose out, it doesn't have to be a particular route. So what we want to focus on is what we believe to be our purpose and why we want what we want fundamentally. Like we used for example, it's to teach not go be a school teacher. There are always more routes than what we are currently seeing. If one way doesn't seem right to you, there's a path to express your purpose a different way. So, lets now dive into the 3 ways to identify your true purpose.

#1 – Early Days

Number one might sound weird but, this is where the answer began to reveal itself. When we look at our inner child, we reflect back to what we want at the core. Go back to when you were a kid and take note of the things you wanted to be. Chances are it was something you would consider nuts like Superman, astronaut, or an acrobat. Once you take note of all the things you wanted to be growing up, you then want to ask yourself, "WHY did I want to be this?" Then, look for the fundamentals amongst them. To use an example, the top 3 things I wanted to be growing up were a princess, a teacher, & a rockstar. I wanted to be this mainly because I love to entertain, educate, and have influence.

Growing up, I tried to block those desires because I thought I wouldn't be able to fulfill them for many reasons. However, as I grew older and became educated on how energy works, who I truly was, and followed my vision in business, I realized that I AM a princess, a teacher and a rockstar! I fulfill my purpose through being a speaker, the founder of the BLIVE movement, YouTuber, mentor and author. I get to entertain people, influence them, and teach them through all of these avenues. I get to fulfill my purpose NOT just through one particular pathway.

Our purpose is fundamental to our lives and the path is just a means to it. Sometimes you will still fall in the same path that you envisioned but we want to look for the fundamentals in what we want because sometimes the universe has a much, MUCH better way of expressing it for us. Plus, as we continue on with our lives, the world is constantly changing so getting caught up in a particular route or industry isn't a smart thing to do anyways. So don't get caught up in needing it to be a particular pathway or even having one at this moment, first just identify what the fundamentals are in your inner child. (Write the answers out to really process through this.)

#2 - It's All About Flow

Once you have identified the principles in what you love doing, take note of the things you either do naturally with little to no effort, or get extremely excited whenever you get to do it. Yes, along the way everybody will have to strengthen skills and gain specialized knowledge around what it is they are doing to better assist in the functionality. However, if you don't already have a flow in what you're working towards, chances are it's not in alignment with who you truly are. This is merely an indicator you are trying to do something in a way that wouldn't serve you the best. When not in flow it can also mean that you may be doing the right action but your beliefs between how things are and should be are out of alignment which we will talk about addressing further in this book. Pay attention to what flows.

#3 - Eliminate Weak Beliefs, Program Yourself with Ones That Serve You

This is a process used to get back into alignment by shifting the way you are perceiving the world through what we will refer to as our "human programming." Our human programming is the way our neurology is currently conditioned. It's our beliefs and habits. In a way we are like robots, we can be programmed to do whatever needed to carry out a particular objective. The difference is, we have free will and we have the ability to self program, leaving us the ability to be, do, and have whatever we want. Our brains are programmed to avoid pain and gain pleasure at all times. So, if we desire something strongly and it brings us a lot of pleasure in life yet, simultaneously, have a belief that feels very painful around obtaining it, our programming will not allow us to obtain it. The things we attach pain and pleasure to are a major factor in what controls our neurology. "Pain" and "pleasure" could mean exactly that or it could also be "unknown" and "known" situations because what is painful to the subconscious portion to our brain is what is unfamiliar. So, this also explains why there is self sabotage in obtaining new goals we so badly desire at a conscious level. Below are a few examples on what a belief may sound like in relation to blocking you from fulfilling your purpose.

" I really want to be a singer but my voice is terrible"

" My family wants me to take this particular route I don't like but I can't let them down"

" I would like to pursue this but, that means I would have no time with my loved ones or self"

" If I decide to go on this path, I will have to do things that don't align with who I am just to be successful"

"My dream is to _____ but very little people ever succeed/nobody is doing it"

" Everybody is doing what I want to do & the competition is ridiculous"

You'll know if a thought occuring inside of you is limiting by the way you are feeling. If you notice some resistance/low vibration in the way you feel, use that as an indicator to know you are thinking a thought out of alignment from being and obtaining that of which you want. Any limiting belief around this will fall into one of four categories.

NOTE HIGH VIBE = JOY, LOVE, PEACE.
LOW VIBE = FEAR, SHAME, GUILT

1)**Acceptance-** whether that be acceptance/love of a partner, of ourselves, friend, family member, public,etc. Fear of abandonment/judgement, need of approval, or to be liked.

2)**Sacrifice-**meaning you have to do something you don't want to do in order to obtain what you want.

3)**Likelihood/Ability-** resources, location, certification, self worth, connections, track record, etc.

4)**Ignorance-** lack of faith, lack of awareness

So, once you have locked in what you believe your purpose to be, ask yourself, "What would my life look/feel like if I lived out my purpose in the most fulfilling way for me? What would my life look/feel like once I obtained what I truly wanted?"

By doing this, you are beginning to train your

human programming to line up with the experience you intend to have. Remember, everything in this world is already created, it's just a matter of aligning your inner reality with that of which you'd like to experience so that you can perceive it in your outer reality. When our inner reality is in alignment with that which we want we can then physically see/hear the things that help us and can carry out the proper thoughts, language, and actions.

To shift our inner reality, the next thing we want to do after identifying our true target, is set an intention for it. Relating back to the Universal Law of Perpetual Transmutation of Energy, intention is the action that transmutes the desire a.k.a "wanting" energy to the "having" energy. As you know from other universal laws stated in previous chapters, we can't experience a reality of having if we are in the vibration of wanting. Those are two different sides of the subject! In my YouTube video, "How to properly set intentions," I walk you through the step by step process in depth on how to properly set an intention. I highly suggest you watch and apply that before you move onto the next chapter. In case you are not able to access/watch YouTube right now, just know that it is merely deciding that this will happen for you or something better no matter what. You expect it. It's making a firm decision, moving out of the wishing state and remaining in certainty on its fruition.

Chapter 3 –
You Literally Had No Idea

So, now that you understand that we must **align our programming a.k.a dominant vibration** to that which we set intentions for in order for us to experience it... The step that comes before any sort of strategy, any sort of physical effort, anything at all, what keeps us from doing so?

Four simple things:

1. **Initial Programming**
2. **Environment**
3. **Habits**
4. **Ignorance**

It's important to address this now so you can understand how you came to your current reality and how it is continuously formed. By knowing this, you also begin to know how, why and when to implement your power. Let us first take a look at how a belief is formed in the first place. A belief begins as a thought and whenever that thought is passed down to the subconscious brain, it becomes an "official" belief. I put quotations around official because we will be discussing how to uproot it and how to intentionally form a belief. To understand even further how a thought gets passed down to the subconscious brain (and formed into a belief) is first by knowing it passses the two levels of brain prior to it, the forebrain and midbrain. The forebrain is what is responsible for our judgement, thinking. The midbrain is what is responsible for our senses.

In order for you to pass a thought down to your subconscious, it's a matter of becoming psychosomatic on the thought. Meaning, we have to incorporate more than just thought. It's about sensory, judgment and feeling as well. This is why affirmations and words alone will not work. There has to be a removal of judgement behind any dominant beliefs that contradict with what you are choosing to now shift into and FEEL the words as if they were true already in order to bypass the first layer of our minds. Immersion of the senses just like it would be if it were "real" - so feeling, tasting, touching, hearing, seeing so it bypasses the second.

This is the phenomenon that happens whenever we "reprogram" ourselves or download any sort of belief. Hypnotherapy is something I perform with my clients due to this reason. Hypnotherapy is a highly leveraged tool to use because it opens up a pathway to the subconscious, almost like a straight download, for the preferred beliefs to go it. However, you will learn how to use many different tools in order to do this. This is also why visualization is essential for us to obtain what we desire. In order for anything to become real, it has to appeal to that form of sensory as well.

Now that you know what happens in order for something to become a belief, let's take a look at how we got to our current programming starting with where it started initially.

#1-Initial Programming

Up until about the age of roughly 7, we are soaking in

everything around us with little to almost no judgement because we are in the beginning development stages of our life. We are just finding our way into the world and haven't yet developed a critical mind to really judge and reason. We are learning everything by having it taught to us. So, our initial human programming is basically a direct reflection of the input around us during those times. You think, dress, eat, talk, everything under the sun, just like the people/place you were brought up in during these times. (That is, until you start deciding otherwise that you want different once the critical mind is developed.) However, do not feel limited by this because you are going to learn how to completely swipe out this programming if you wish and why your DNA doesn't even matter.

#2-Environment

We are the ones who ultimately choose how we think, feel, act. We are the ones who have the power to ultimately choose what our conditioning is like & how we perceive the world. That is free will. Our environment though, has a very strong influence over what frequency our vibration is at. Environment meaning everything outside us- the people, lights, smells, everything. So, it's important that we are aware of this so we aren't subliminally hypnotized. Remember, all it takes is for a thought to bypass those first two layers of the brain & it becomes a part of your conditioning.

In fact, many times of the day we fall into a hypnotic state without even realizing it, causing us to become brainwashed by our surrounding environment when not aware. This typically happens when we are driving, learning, or feeling an overload of emotion (especially stress).

When it comes to people, we are influenced by the need to be loved/accepted and by what everybody else is doing. By denying this, you are doing yourself a disservice. We all are, it's the way humans are set up so that we can co-exists. When you accept it for what it is, you have the power to let it not influence you because you are now aware that you will be naturally pulled to it. For most people, the fear of judgement or the need to be liked is far stronger than their own personal desires. As you know from an earlier segment, the brain is always looking to avoid pain and gain pleasure. This is one reason why people are influenced by others. Another is because we have to learn how to survive if we want to live and one of the ways humans learn is through mirroring. We look to see how other humans are doing things to give us clarity on what to do. It's a by-product to be naturally influenced by what the masses are doing if you're not consciously aware of the influence.

Color, light, and sound all have very tricky ways of influencing us. As a matter of fact, everything breaks down to sound and/or light. Your vibration is literally a sound, you could put it onto a record and it would play a song. Your belief system could literally be put into a soundtrack. The frequency of each sound determines what the actual object or thing is resonating with.

Now, most people are aware of the fact that language, people, and music influences the way we feel. However, most people are unaware of how deeply each subject can have an influence on us. For example, the color of somebody's shirt could determine whether or not you resonate with one being trustworthy or not because of the subconscious influence of color. Music and instruments, when used with good intention, can easily help us reach high vibrational states of being, coasting our mind into operating in a way we'd like it to be. However, most sound being put out there isn't intended to raise your frequency. Most of the music and noise you hear on a regular basis actually keeps you TRAPPED in a low frequency state of being. Reason being is, our brain waves are linking to sound. Since every sound is on a frequency, what we are choosing to resonate with, "tune into", determines what we are perceiving and receiving in our experience. Our brain waves determine how we are thinking and what we are even capable to tune into! Remember though, your consciousness is in power so, the more aware of these things you become, the less subliminal effect they will have. Do not be afraid of these things, just be aware. Stay conscious. You always have the power to be in control.

#3-Habits

Here is where the potency resides in what we are putting out and receiving in. What are you in the habit of? One of the dominant ways our body and minds learn is through repetition. When it comes to aligning our inner reality to the reality we prefer to experience, are we in the habit of doing so? Are we in the habit of using things like emotional intelligence, remaining conscious of any unserving influence, being aware of any perceived limitation we are coming across so that we can realign ourselves? When we are in the habit of doing these things, we are a person who is predominately in alignment with the reality you prefer to experience- allowing it to actually manifest into your life.

#4-Ignorance

The biggest reason why people don't have their programming, their vibration, in alignment with what they would like to experience is because they are not in the habit of doing so. If they were in the habit of doing so, they would be experiencing it involuntarily at times. People are only not in the habit of doing this simply due to ignorance. Whether that be ignorance of how this works or the ignorance of how to form a habit in a way that is enticing for them, isn't a drag. The purpose of this book is to teach you how to identify the vibration of what you truly desire and how to develop habits that allow you shift into the identity (shift into the consistent vibration of) of the person who experiences that reality in a way that allows you to be truly fulfilled. So, by the end of this book, you will know how to SMASH all of these "barriers" and leverage them to your advantage.

The purpose of this book from here on out is to teach you how to exactly apply this knowledge now that you have got back in touch with your true, limitless, purpose-filled desires. Remember, this book is for the personal transformation you want at this point in your life, so we will be speaking about that in context. However, the same principles discussed in this book can be applied in obtaining anything you desire. This is what happens whenever we manifest, this *is* what takes place in order for *any* manifestation to occur. This is what is happening all the time whether you consciously do it or not. This is determining what you are currently perceiving in your now "reality." Every moment is a manifestation. With that being said, take these principles and go on to achieve many things. Take these principles and teach them to other people so that they can do the same with their lives and goals. #BLIVE

Now that you are clear on how your current programming/vibration came to be, how it is continuously formed, and what reality you truly would like for it to correspond to, it's time to start shifting into that experience! But first let your fellow BLIVERS, the ones consciously creating their life experience as well, know what you set intentions for and are excited about! By applying the lessons taught in this book, in this community you will be able to find & link with the people that will help you fulfill your mission and support you all the way.

www.facebook.com/groups/blivemovement

Chapter 4 – It's All About Matching

Okay, so now what? You know what it is you truly want and what you believe to be your purpose. You transmuted the desire, the "wanting" energy, into an intention. You set the intention that you are going through this transformation RIGHT NOW but, now what? How do we actually *DO* that? How do we co-create with universal laws and shift our vibration to experience the things we set intentions for? It's simple, just grab a S.A.C.! LOL. (**subtract, add & connect.**)

"Add" as in open up the neural pathways, the stimulation, the feelings that allow you to be in the vibration of what you desire. "Subtract" as in close off the neural pathways, the beliefs, the habits that cause you to be in the vibration less of what you truly want. "Connect" as in expand your consciousness and relation with all that is and all that you are so that you remain in frequency.

As we address this part of the discussion, it's important to remind you that you are not "fixing" yourself. We are eliminating blockages from all that we truly are and have available to us. In this modern day, so many people are focused on "fixing" what's wrong - the reprogramming. The problem is, just like we had stated earlier about being in the wanting and having state, they are opposite ends of the stick.

So when people are coming from a place of needing to "fix", they simultaneously aren't in the vibration of that which they want. This book is only called "Reinvent Yourself" because we live in a world where we are dominated by influence for the need to be better. When under that influence, "better" is what other people determined and then you accept it as truth. The best thing you can not only do for yourself but, the world around you, is be truly you & live out the purpose you came here for. That is why in the introduction and again now I am stressing to you that you are actually removing your shadow on who you truly are by "reinventing yourself."

Reprogramming will happen as a by-product whenever we are focusing and acting in alignment with the vibration of that which we desire. It is only needing to be addressed when our emotional intelligence signals to us that there is work needing to take place in the present moment. We want to spend most of our time focusing on what we do want and always matching the vibration of that. However, I am going to be giving you a list of tools to use in order to reprogram yourself whenever necessary in the moment.

Matching Vibration

Let's dive in! In order to shift into the experience we set intentions for, we have to identify the vibration of what we are shifting to.

So how do we know the vibration of something? Let us first bring it back to what makes up our vibration and how to know when it's alignment with our target. Our vibration consists of our mental, emotional, and physical plane. Using emotional intelligence (a.k.a. observing and being aware of the meaning of our emotions), we will be able to find out if our vibration is in alignment with that which we set intentions for. When our current vibration is aligned with what we desire, we feel great - in "flow." We are in high frequency states of being like love, joy, peace. This state of being is what allows us to carry out the proper thoughts, feelings and actions that then allow us to perceive and receive our intended manifestations.

We know when our vibration is out of alignment with our desire whenever we feel off from these high vibrational states of being. No matter what triggered the shift in the vibration, first will come out of alignment thought, then emotion, then (hopefully not but happens if not adjusted) out of alignment action. That is why "emotional intelligence" is a thing. Emotions are a signal and when you become aware of what they truly mean for you, you then have the opportunity to consciously shift your vibration to be back into alignment with that which you desire.

Even though we have the ability to shift our vibration whenever pleased, you know from reading this book that our vibration is whatever energetic frequency we are dominantly resonating at in the moment. Because of that, we keep referring to programming because that is where the real leverage is at referring to that statement. This is true because our subconscious mind (a.k.a. our programming) is what is running the show for roughly 90% of your life.

For most people, their conscious vibration is different from their subconscious vibration. When that is true for somebody, you can now see why they consciously could be doing all the right things but never end up getting the true results they want. If somebody isn't experiencing that which they desire on a consistent basis, it's because their programming (a.k.a. consistent vibration) isn't in alignment with it.

Our subconscious programming, or our subconscious vibration, is what is engraved into us neurologically due to intensity (strong emotion), consistency (habits) and what we are associating to based off of memory. When we are in consciousness, we have the ability to judge, reason, *CHANGE*, a belief/story we are picking up on --even if it's been engraved into us our whole lives. When we use consciousness in an intended way, we have the ability to literally change the direction our cells are communicating to each other, thereby, forming new neural pathways and changes in our DNA. This is what then causes new thoughts, feelings, and actions (a.k.a. new vibration) resulting in new life experience. You already started to learn how to do some of this based on earlier context.

So what's the vibration of that which you set intentions for? Let's look at the chart below. You will always have the answer by using your emotional intelligence. You will be in a high vibration. You will be in "flow" state. You will be in knowing, faith. That is alignment. Anytime we feel anything other than that, it's because we are thinking something that will cause us to perceive, speak and act in a way that doesn't allow us to align with our desires.
Emotion is a signal that something is off or we are on the right path. We first can determine it with being aware of what our bodies and minds are telling us. That is leveraging your emotions and using emotional intelligence.

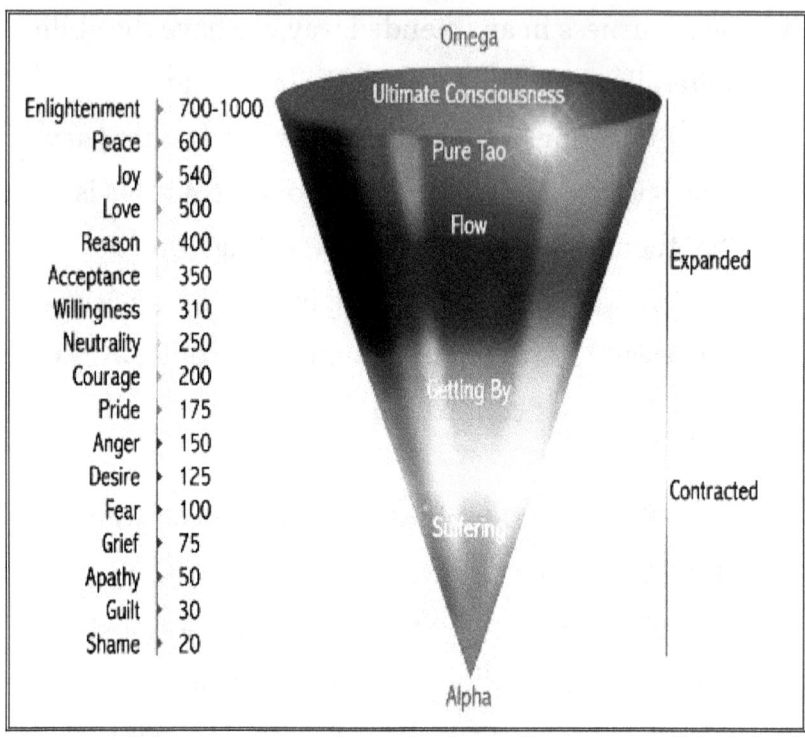

If you were to all of a sudden step into the reality of experiencing everything you truly desire, you want to ask yourself: "How am I thinking, feeling, and acting in these present moments?" This is where we use our imagination very psychosomatically and ask ourselves questions around these topics. When we get into such a strong state of imagination, our subconscious mind actually thinks it's real and so you are legitimately identifying the vibration of something when are you doing this. Below, I have listed a series of questions for you to answer to help you to identify the vibration of your intentions. There is also an exercise that teaches you how to properly visualize so that you can step into this vibration more psychosomatically.

If you had already begun to imagine and ask yourself what you would be thinking, feeling, and acting like if you had just walked into that reality, you might start to realize some contradiction in the way you feel and think right now.

You may have started to say, "I'd be doing this but, that also means I'd be doing _____"; "I would feel this way but ___"; or "I can't until _____."

These are the types of thoughts that cause us to not be in the vibration and not develop the programming that aligns with our desires. We are going to be talking about exactly how to reprogram these thought patterns but for now, just focus on identifying the vibration you set intentions for. Don't worry, it's completely normal for a ton of contradiction to come up but, gently dismiss it and turn your attention back to what you are intending to experience for yourself. To do so, all we have to do is get into a grounded state of being, let our limitless imagination take over, and ask ourselves questions that help us connect to what is.

Remember, *we first become* what we want to experience and then our external reality will *reflect* it to us. Visualization isn't just an optional tool, it's REQUIRED! As I stated earlier, our experiences are created in our minds before we experience them. Even before we get somewhere, we create the picture in our mind as to what it's going to be like and how we think it's going to play out. We get what we expect and so we want to intentionally visualize that which we want and not let our programming takeover based upon what you'd normally expect before reading this book. You don't need to know all the details as there other external factors are at play. However, you do want to identify what you want to experience and how to train your mind what to expect, therefore align with.

The Reticular Activating System

Our eyes are picking up OVER MILLIONS pixels of information at once. To keep us focused and create the experience we want, the Reticular Activating System is responsible for filtering out anything "unimportant" leaving you with the only physical interpretation of UP TO 200 PIXELS. That is an EXTREME amount of information we are legitimately blind to every waking moment of our lives. A similar concept happens with our ears, which is why people seem to have "selective hearing." So, the key is training the mind and body as to what really is "important" so that way you can be laser focused and perceive opportunities/solutions RIGHT IN FRONT OF YOU.

      As we ask ourselves these upcoming questions, we want to envision ourselves already living in the reality we are intending for. We don't even want to envision ourselves doing it from a standpoint like "that will be so nice when _____" or "I can't wait until _____." Even though they are positive, these are all points of view that are not already in obtainment, not already experiencing the desires we set intentions for.

Before asking yourself the questions, we are going to go through a quick visualization exercise that helps you connect deeper to your intended vibration. I also have a video series on my YouTube channel which discusses diving deep into visualization. You can find it simply by typing in "Elizabeth Otis Visualization."

www.youtube.com/elizabethotis

Visualization Steps

Get Grounded
Drown out any internal and external noise, quiet the mind & become neutral

Set The Intention
This is where you now give yourself "permission" to step into your new reality without letting any contradictory energy interfere.

Make it Psychosomatic

In order for anything to become "real" our judgement has to say so and it be sensory incorporated. We surpass any judgment by step number two so, now it is a matter of linking our senses to complete the experience of it.

Give Gratitude and Enjoy

Our subconscious brain doesn't know what's real and what's not. Anything that gets to it becomes real until further change is made. So, if you have completed the above steps successfully, give yourself a moment to enjoy this current, delusional yet soon to be true, space in time. Giving gratitude is the cherry on top to carrying out a proper visualization and matching the vibration to our desires because gratitude is the ultimate "receiving state." When we give thanks, it's because we feel we have been given something. So when we feel gratitude for what we are visualizing, we are teaching ourselves that this is real, we are receiving it.

Remember: the more you do this, the more you are shaping your programming how to be. We will be discussing how to incorporate programming habits into our daily rituals so that by the end of this book you are habitually doing the things that allow you to not just experience your now intentions but, every new desired experience to come. This is a fundamental equation.

Moving on to the Vibration Matching Questions

You will want to really gain a deeper understanding of what it *feels* like for you. As you are in the successful state of visualization, you will want to ask yourself the following questions...

ACTIONS
- How is my physiology?
- How is my body posture?
- How am I treating my health?
- What environment am I choosing to surround myself in?
- What places do I go to?
- Who are the types of people I involve myself with?
- What are my daily activities like?
- What do I wear?
- How do I interact with people?

THOUGHTS
- How am I speaking to myself?
- What do I think about myself?
- How do I view the way I am showing up in the world?
- How do I view the world?
- How do I view other people?
- How do I view the way I interact with other people and my environment?

FEELINGS
- How does this make me feel? What does this feel like?

These are the two questions you ask when it comes to feeling because any question around feeling will fall in those categories.

***** FEELING is what we want to pay the *most* attention to once we have completed the above questions. What's most important is our feelings. The state we are in IS the connection that takes the cord (you) and plugs you into the socket (frequency of what you desire.) OUR STATE IS EVERYTHING.

You do not need to have the answers to all of these questions, nor do you need to have everything figured out. The purpose of the above exercises are to help you identify *what it feels like* whenever you are in alignment with that of which you want so that you can carry that vibration over into your dominant way of being.

(Don't try to be perfect about identifying the vibration, go general for now if you need to.)

The above exercises simultaneously help train our neurology to serve us in experiencing our desires by getting us more familiar with them. Remember, the more familiar something is, the more pleasurable it is to our subconscious. The more pleasurable something is to our subconscious, the more our programming will work tirelessly to bring it into our experience. Now that you have identified what it feels like whenever you are in the vibrational state of being of what it is you want, what it feels like to be in alignment, it's time to learn how to program yourself to have it as your dominant state of being. As you learned earlier, our programming is influenced by dominancy (intense emotion), consistency (habits), and the associations we have based off of memory.

Dominancy is a byproduct of truly utilizing the tools in this book because when you truly are making something psychosomatic the emotional intensity is there. You can feel it as real to the point where tears of joy come out, you feel completely uplifted, at peace. The reason why we don't want to just incorporate dominancy and not consistency (or the other way around) is because if we take a look at the analogy of keeping a moat up on the beach, you can make it as giant or deep as you want but, eventually, the consistent pounding of the waves will smooth it over. Same goes with the opposite -- if the goal was to keep leveled sand on the beach but everytime the waves finally smoothed it over another giant moat was dug, there would still always be a moat. In order for there to be a **REAL** change, there has to be both dominant emotion and consistent habits/experiences. At the end of this segment, you will have a toolbelt full of things to do to help you immerse yourself in the vibration of that which you want so that it becomes a part of your programming.

Also, in most cases, to even receive our desires initially, our vibration must be consistent for a cycle of time while there is little to no external evidence showing that says otherwise. Due to the Law of Gestation, your vibration must be consistently (for the most part) in alignment with your intentions because this law states that in order for something to come into fruition, a process, a cycle is involved. If your vibration is choppy during this cycle, you are constantly throwing yourself back and forth on different paths within the present moment. This is also why our vibration must be consistent in order to keep what we have obtained as well. Since our subconscious vibration is what is taking over the majority of the time, if we obtain something in alignment consciously but don't align subconsciously, we will lose it. You can now see why the leverage is in shifting your programming to match that of which you want.

You are not here to learn how to just have magical moments of manifestation when you're on a high cloud. You are learning how to be habitually in alignment with the reality you desire so that you can intentionally live a fulfilling life for yourself due to having this formula down pat. This is so much more than "success habits." This is the science that allows you to inevitably link up with that which you desire using your own personal power, your energy... a way of living that allows you to be free & limitless because you know you can always get what you want when you link up to it.

Chapter 5 – Who's The Captain In Control?

Now I know you get the idea that you will want to be in that vibration majority of the time; or that there's no exact "time" that you want to be this vibration. You get that this is a new way of living, a new culture for you. By knowing that, you also get that you are breaking old habits. So, if you don't hold yourself to a higher standard until it's in automation, this knowledge just remains in your memory and you don't see any result from it. You are forming new neural pathways, so there will be some discomfort and resistance at times. With that being said, overtime these habits will become an automation and you'll become addicted to doing the things that empower you. Also, by experiencing any resistance on something you know is good for you, you want to use your emotional intelligence to find out what meaning you are linking to that subject so that you can change the perspective to serve you.

Rituals are what get us in the habit of doing something. We already have our own set of rituals and so it's just a matter of adding a few tweaks to what you are already doing to get you into alignment. Almost everything we do is a habit. To begin shifting your rituals in a way that develops new programming, we will focus first on quick, but powerful tools that allow us to do this. Then, we will focus on how you can incorporate these rituals in your individual lifestyle. That being said, let's discuss how to use the tools provided and how they work to shift our neurology and state of being. Some of them are self explanatory and so we'll just discuss the why on those.

REFLECT/TRACK/ DAILY
- Meditate
- Flow/Movement of The Body
- Read/Study
- Visualize
- Affirmations of your Highest & Best Self

- Gratitude
- Appreciation
- Ask the "Good" Questions
- Connect Spiritually
- Connection (like minded)
- Proper Nutritional/Fluid Needs
- Grounding In Nature
- Silence
- Fun
- Set Intentions
- Shadow Work
- Breath Work
- Celebrate
- Reflect
- Belief Breakthrough
- Hypnosis
- Binaural Beats
- Journaling
- Set Environment Up For Success
- GDG Sandwich

Set Intentions

Based on earlier chapters, you already know how to properly set intentions and that it is the action that transmutes the desire (wanting) energy into experience (having) energy. In earlier exercises, you already set the general intention to shift into the reality of your desire. Daily, you will want to do this exercise for the actionable steps to get you there for that given day. Start living your life under intended outcomes. When you wake up, set an intention to fulfill your missions for that given day.

For example, when you walk into a room, set an intention for your desired outcome for when you have left. When you go to call somebody, set an intention for how you want to phone call to go. You want to set as many intentions as you can. However, remember to not become attached to the outcomes for infinite intelligence knows best and sometimes will give us something different instead. When we become attached, we start shifting back to the "desiring" or "wanting" side of the stick which is the opposite side we want to be on.

Connect Spirituality

Everybody has their own "source." Whether that be a particular religion, universe, creator, or simply just themselves. Whatever it is for you, it's important we connect to it daily because this connection is what allows you to embrace all that is as one, feel true love, and access infinite intelligence.

Visualize

You already now know how to properly visualize and the science behind it based off of earlier chapters. So, this is merely a reminder to get you in the *habit* of visualizing. For anything to ever become real to your subconscious, it just has to go through the first couple layers of the brain. Once it's a part of our subconscious, it becomes our vibration for the majority of the time. Remember, we get what we expect... what our vibration is. So, engrave your intentions with visualization. Also, here is another reminder about the fact that you have any RAS... the more you visualize something, the more you are training it to show you exactly what it is you truly want.

Affirmations

This section is a little longer but, it's very simple. Affirmations are what become our beliefs, part of our vibration. There are myths around affirmations and extremely wrong ways to use them, which makes sense as to why some people don't think they work. The thing is, everything is an affirmation because everything is affirming to you as to how or why something works the way it does. Our language matters big time but, remember everything is first sound so, it doesn't matter so much the words themselves, it matters the vibration of them. With that being said, the way you feel when you speak is the most important factor to affirmations. There is a particular way to structure affirmations so that it triggers your brain and body to operate, therefore feel, a certain way. So, to know how to leverage on the benefit of auto-suggestion and power of language, there are just 3 steps to structure an affirmation by.

#1 – Triple P- Positive, Personal, Present

Positive meaning ONLY focusing on the subject/thing/experience that you want and NOT the things you don't want. Example: "I am surrounded by loving people" vs. "I am far away from negativity." You never want to use the words of what you DON'T want in your life because words like " don't, not, without " don't really register to our brains. They just pick up the **keywords.** So, we want to direct our attention only on what we want.

Personal meaning "I" statements.- not any control over other people/things. Example: "I attract loving people", "I am easily loved everywhere I am" or "My vibration puts me in the experience of loving people" vs "People are loving towards me." We only have control over our personal experience because everybody has free will. However, the frequency of your vibration determines how you experience people interacting with you.

Lastly, going back to what we discussed in Chapter One, "time" isn't real. The only time that exists is now and it's the only "time" our subconscious knows! So, we must step into the "now" present state of obtaining it. Now, there are two ways to structure a statement in present form. The first way is already in obtaining it. The second way is in the process of obtaining it. Now, I know that sounds contradicting but, here are some examples…"I am surrounded by loving people" or "I am meeting a lot of loving people." They key to know the difference in whether you should structure it already in obtainment or in the process of it is to go by rule #2 of structuring affirmations.

#2 – Feeling

Rule #2 is to GO by feeling! Incorporate it AND let it guide you. Remember, in order for anything to be passed down to our subconscious, the experience has to be psychosomatic. Affirmations can actually harm you if you aren't letting your emotions guide you in using them. There is a video on my YouTube channel going over that if you want to know more about that branch of information. It doesn't matter so much what you are actually saying moreover how you are feeling. The reason we structure our words in a particular way is because of the way it triggers the human brain to operate. However, pay even closer attention to feeling. When you say the first option of affirmations, claiming it as already done, and you notice some resistance/disbelief/gutcheck when you say it, then don't use that option. If that's you, then use the "in the process of" structure of the affirmation. They are both still present, one just may be easier for you to feel into depending on where your current belief system is at. Remember, if you choose the 2nd option, it wouldn't sound like "I am in the process of doing this one day", it would sound like "I am currently on the journey of." Pay attention to the way you feel when you structure these because you don't want to create additional resistance for yourself. Whatever option you choose will not determine the speed at which you actually experience it. What will determine how fast you get there is the energy you have behind it so always go with what has least resistance.

#3 - Pain/Pleasure

Lastly, remember that all of our actions are based on doing something to gain pleasure and avoid pain. So, structure your thoughts, affirmations, your beliefs, in a MAGNETIC way! What seems more exciting: "I attract loving people" or " I attract energetic, crazy fun, loving people who want to live life just like me?" Clearly the second option. So spice it up a little. Remember, YOU CAN HAVE IT ALL!!!! Anything is achievable under the following universal laws. So, don't limit yourself, GO BIG! This is why the BLIVE movement was created & the BLIVERS in our community say, "Dream Big, Live Large! **#BLIVE** You set limitless intentions for your true desires, true dreams, and live out that in a way that fulfills you to extreme satisfaction. DREAM BIG, so that you can LIVE LARGE, and simply BLIVE. BLIVE by being a conscious creator, intentionally manifesting your own reality. The clay is in your hand. Sculpt it however you want my friend.

Gratitude

Gratitude is for many reasons. Yes, all the obvious ones like being thankful, showing appreciation etc. However, let's talk about the science of gratitude and what happens neurologically when we give it. When we give gratitude for something, we experience more of it for a couple of reasons.

1 — Being that, the more attention we put on something the more it grows.

2 - Being that, when we give gratitude for something, it's because we believe we have been given something- being in gratitude is an ultimate receiving state. So, give gratitude for what has already happened but, give gratitude for the blessings that are to come! Say thank you in advance for experiencing the intentions you set out for self. This literally is teaching your subconscious that you already have it. Remember, feeling is KEY in all of these tools! Giving appreciation will also raise your personal vibration by shifting your focus!

Appreciation

Appreciation is similar to gratitude but, it is still a different tool to use. We give gratitude to give thanks, we feel appreciation to simply admire. When we spend time admiring something, we create more of it in our lives. It's as simple as that. The Law of Attraction states that we get what we focus on. Our subconscious mind does whatever it can to remain around things that are "familiar" because what's familiar is pleasurable to it. The more we appreciate, the more familiar it becomes.

Appreciation itself also raises your vibration through changing the body's chemistry, neurological communication, and overall bioelectromagnetic field (aura.)

Ask the "Good" Questions

Our brain will give us an answer to any question that we ask it, even if it is not true. For example, you could be anorexic but if you ask yourself the question "why am I so fat?" your self-talk will say something like "because you're lazy" or "because you need to work out more." So, we want to become aware of the questions we are asking ourselves, making sure they aren't negative generalizations like "why is this so hard for me?" or "why does this always happen to me?", & ONLY ask ourselves the "Good Questions." The "Good Questions" are the ones that come from "everything is for my benefit" frame of mind and/or questions that already assume you have what you want. Examples such as-

- "How can I leverage this?"
- "How does this grow me as a person?"
- "What opportunity did this birth?"
- "Why do I have such a fulfilling life?"
- "Why do I have such a successful life?"
- "Why do I have everything I could possibly need and want?"
- "Why am I surrounded by so much love?"

By asking these questions, it forces our mind to come up with an answer for it therefore leaving you either **A-**steps to take or **B-** attention towards what was already there that you weren't seeing. Always be sure to be asking yourself the "Good Questions."

Proper Fluid + Nutritional Needs

This isn't here just because it's healthy again. Your physiology pretty much works one in the same with the way you are thinking and feeling. Based off of earlier chapters, you know this to be true already with posture and expressions. It is true for the internal side of things, too. If your blood sugar levels, for example, are all over the place it's going to throw your vibration out of whack because your body keeps signaling to you that it needs something. Yes, you can overcome your mood with your mentality but, this bleeds into the way we can even operate and your energy levels, thereby your willpower. The average person doesn't even drink the recommended amount of water in a day, let alone nourish themselves properly, leaving the average person walking around lacking the full opportunity to operate at their potential because they aren't properly taking care of their nutritional and fluid needs. Make a conscious effort to eat clean, high vibrational foods and get the proper amount of vitamins/minerals/fluids each and everyday.

We are only able to take in a certain number of message units per day before our body begins to shut down. The number of message units we can handle (message units being all light/sound frequencies) is extremely impacted by our diet.

Also, you are what you eat. The energy of the food you ingest goes through the Law of Perpetual Transmutation of Energy inside of you. Different foods have different levels of vibration to them, then those vibrations transmute into you when you eat it. **Rule of thumb to go by:** the more natural and plant based it is, the higher the vibration. Note: meat and dairy products are some of the worst things you can eat in terms of vibration because of the fear and trauma energy inside of it. If you need motivation to go vegetarian, at the very least, just do some research on the slaughtering industry. Also, see for yourself how majority of these animals are forced to live and be treated. That alone is gut wrenching enough if you know what actually happens in most industries. Can you imagine being hung upside down by your feet and having your throat slit till you bleed out and die? That's what some of these animals go through.

Plus, knowing what you know now about transmutation of energy, the energy of fear and trauma from the killed animals gets put into you when you eat them. This is why people who eat a lot of meat tend to have more anger. You can also raise the vibration of the food and water you put into your system (before ingested) by simply using transmutation of energy over them by prayer of gratitude or power of intention. This is why food prepared by somebody who has a lot of love or passion (like grandma) tends to taste better. Yes, because of their skills but, most importantly the energy they transmuted into it whether they realize they did it or not. You can't help to feel good because you just ingested love energy through the food. Crazy, right?

One last thing to also take note of is an alkaline diet. **Get this information out everywhere!** CANCER CANNOT LIVE IN AN ALKALINE

ENVIRONMENT!! Neither can a boatload of other health issues. When you have an alkaline based diet, not only are you healthier but, you also think clearer, you have more energy, and you LOOK better. It's sickening but, the only reason why this information hasn't gotten out yet is because of all of the systems built & based around the health & beauty industries. This is also the same reason why you didn't know you could heal yourself with your mind and body only. Yes, you can literally shift your entire life experience with your **mind and body**. If everybody knew this, 90% of industries, systems, and programs would crumble because it dismisses everything we have been led to believe our entire lives on how things "work" and "have to be." Having an alkaline based diet helps keep you in alignment and your vibration high because the foods itself have a high vibration, it allows you to focus, and it's 10x easier to keep your energy high with this diet vs an acidic diet.

Silence

Silence is powerful because it allows us to observe and really be conscious of not only what's going on around us but, within us. Going back to the way our brain waves work with the way we think, silence allows us to slip back to a state of being that allows us to observe what's going on within. From this state of being, we can make intuitive decisions, become clear, receive answers and be aware of any limitation. Practicing silence is really just that, practicing silence. Get in a place where there isn't much movement going on and just observe what's really going on in your thought process. (Side note - if you begin to fall into a negative thought pattern, switch to a focused state of appreciation.)

Breath Work

Breath work is extremely important because it has numerous direct health benefits and most importantly, directs the way we are thinking and feeling. Deep, full breaths allow us to be in a clear minded, peaceful state. While shallow and short breaths induce stress, anxiety, and tension. Most people aren't breathing deep, full breaths. They are holding their breath when performing tasks throughout the day, depriving themselves of the benefits from breathing fully. It is recommended that throughout the day you become conscious of the way you are breathing and do a check on yourself to see if you are breathing deep, full breaths or quick, shallow, short breaths and correct your breathing patterns whenever necessary. There is also a free video series on my YouTube channel on different breath work techniques.

Meditation

We all know what meditation is and if you need help on learning how to do so, I do have guides in our BLIVE community free for your benefit. So, this is a reminder for you to start incorporating it into your daily rituals. Meditation is to raise our frequency, to become the master of ourselves, open up our consciousness, heal ourselves, and be in alignment with who we truly are. Meditation is a tool that is highly recommended to start in daily use to align yourself. I used to discredit this because I am such an energetic person and it just seemed not as important because I didn't know the true purpose of it. I thought it was just to "chill out." When you intentionally meditate to do the following above, you transform any shadow into the pure, infinite bright energy you are;

exposing you to the limitless creation ability you've always had inside.

Grounding in Nature

As you know from chapter one, everything is energy. Therefore, we are nothing but a bunch of energy that holds a particular charge. By getting out in raw nature, perferably barefoot, you neutralize and draw out any non serving energy from your person. Stressed? Get out in nature. Transmutation of energy is always taking place and so since nature is pure, it takes away impurities. Get out in nature everyday. If you live in the city, get more plants in your home and connect with them. Do not substitute the real experience for watching the nature channel or with fake plants. It's not the same energy force.

(P.S. Let this be an inspiration for you to help go plant trees for our world and buy land for conservation!! Help raise the vibration of the overall planet by doing this!)

Flow/Movement of The Body

Going back to physiology. We want to make sure our

physiology is on point. On point as in its alignment with the person who experiences that which you set the intentions for. You don't have to lift weights, run, or even go to the gym but, you do want to be physical each and every day, remaining active. If you keep your body in little to no motion, in addition to all the health benefits you are depriving yourself of, you also are depriving yourself from simply being in a high vibration. Remember, our physiology commands the way we feel. Have fun with this. It could be as simple as incorporating time to dance every single day. Keep it in alignment by not just doing something in the morning or evening, have an active life where you let energy flow through your body on a continuous basis. Stay aware of the state of being your body posture and facial expressions are triggering you to feel as well. If you work where you have to sit a lot, take frequent breaks to get up and move and shake. Dance in your chair, shake in your seat, do something to keep the energy flowing through your body. Stagnant physiology induces stagnant feeling. Are you smiling? Are your eyes feeling bright? Is your back straight? Always remember not to exclude the body portion from being in alignment! This will also help keep your overall energy levels up, your head space clear, and of course you will be healthier.

Read/Study/Learn/Expand

What are you filling your cup with? As we walk around and live life, we are absorbing everything around us. Since the majority of the world isn't, yet, consciously creating their reality, you have a lot of garbage bombarding your energy throughout your day. Things like the media, limited thinking people, subliminal propaganda, overall low-vibe environment. It's your job to make sure that your energy is clear and that you are overpowering any external influence by filling your own cup with the information you feel is best for you. By doing this, you are intentionally keeping your programming set in a way that you prefer instead of letting it be mutated by your environment. You're doing that now by reading this book, congratulate yourself for that! As you begin to shift your overall vibration more and more, you'll feel even more inspired to dig into particular subjects to grow and expand yourself even further & the ideas you have.

Fun

You might see this part and discredit it. I get that, it doesn't seem as important as the tactical tools for change. Here's the thing though, going back to the way our humans work, we are always trying to avoid pain and gain pleasure. So, when we involve ourselves in something that's really good for us, we will still sabotage ourselves if it's completely boring, draining, if we can't find solutions to really have fun in the process. Adding outside fun to your already schedule is crucial and you definitely, definitely want to find a way to link fun or have fun in the activities you are involving yourself in. This also allows you to become addicted and excited over them through time.

Connect Loved Ones

Introvert, extrovert. It doesn't matter. Humans NEED connection. When we connect with others, we have the opportunity to give, serve, be understood, and feel love with one another. So, if you don't want to call or be around somebody on a particular day, you want to at least connect with the people you love and care about mentally by sending out an energetic message. This will help give you your sense of connection even if they aren't physically there. You can also do this with loved ones who have transitioned.

Connect W/ Like-Minded

Just as we discussed in the previous paragraph, we as humans need that connection. HOWEVER, we don't want to be just connecting with anybody. As I'm sure you know, some people are very toxic to your wellbeing at this time. However, so are a lot of other people without you realizing it because they really aren't doing anything "wrong." The reason I say this is because the Law Of Perpetual Transmutation of Energy is always taking place. We as humans, have a bioelectromagnetic field around us that you can't see but it is made up of our personal vibration. You might have heard of it being called an "aura." When we are around people, even without talking, this energy can transmute together if you aren't being aware of it and protecting your energy field. Therefore, leaving you to take on their energetic qualities until you transmute them out again. This action is taking place before our eyes and we are blind to it. So, be aware and surround yourself with people who have energy you want to be around. **(Note- our bioelectromagnetic fields stick out over 7ft.)**

Also, most people that disagree with you really aren't trying to ever cause you harm, they literally think they are helping you. When you are around people that aren't like minded, they tend to offer their "advice" because your way of thinking seems like an irrational approach to them. You know now that you are a human sponge soaking in everything around you and in order for anything to become a part of your identity, your reality, a truth for you, you have to resonate with that message or image. A lot of times we don't think we are being influenced by people because we consciously disagree but, the more and more we hear something, the more familiar it becomes and the more we resonate and try to make sense out of it.

Also, we are subliminally more influenced by particular figures in our lives and are more suggestible to information during certain times of interaction, no matter who it is, like eating, being taught something, or being around somebody while you are naked. So, it is very polluting to be around people who don't share the same energy as you or where you want to be, even if they are a "good" person and/or don't even say anything to you.

This doesn't necessarily mean you have to stop associating with certain people, you always have to power to protect your energy but, you definitely want to limit your time with them as you become more suggestible to the influence the more you are around it. Also, if you know somebody who you believe holds contradictory energy to you but means all peace, you can introduce them to this material so that they can then personally clean up their own energy and thrive personally as well.

Celebrate

This is different from having fun. Celebration is the conscious acknowledgement for the effort you have put out, wisdom you have acquired, the strength you have, all the amazing that is you. If you're reading a book like this, you are probably somebody who doesn't celebrate themselves enough. I get that things aren't the way you want them to be. I get that you feel like you should have completely different results than you do now and so that there's no real reason to celebrate, I get that 10,000%. The thing is, by not celebrating ourselves we hurt ourselves MORE. If you are in a position where you feel like you shouldn't celebrate yourself, you are one who NEEDS to celebrate yourself.

    Hear me out, it's not allowing yourself to settle or to fake being impressed. Everything happens for a reason and we get what we focus on. So, if we haven't got what we want yet, it's for a REASON and you cannot get to the beneficial side of that if you are focusing on how you missed a goal or how things aren't lining up the way you intended them to be. You could have done everything absolutely right and infinite intelligence had a better outcome for you, so that could be why you didn't get what you expected due to that purpose. No matter what the cause was, you can not see the real purpose and reap the benefits without celebrating yourself because you are not in a clear-minded, "everything happens for my benefit" frame of mind when thinking that way. Make it a ritual to celebrate and acknowledge yourself daily - even if you didn't leave the house.

Also, celebration is NECESSARY for you to form new habits and stick to them. Unconsciously, you give yourself some sort of reward or acknowledgement everytime you follow through on an action or are led to one. We only take action when there is a reward, that's the science of a human. It could be as simple as saying "YES!" or "Good Job" after we complete something but, there is always some sort of reward. Every action can be explained through the Triple R.

Reminder, Routine & Reward

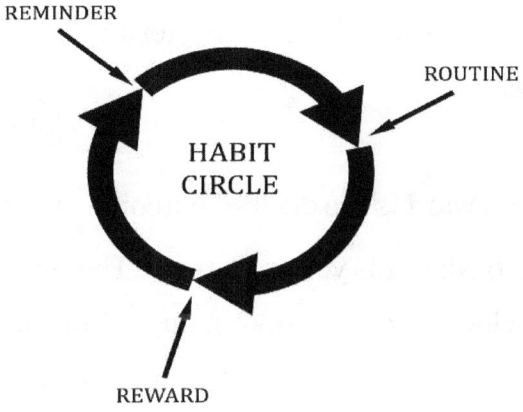

1. What happens first is the "reminder." This is your prompt to take action. Whether that be the alarm going off, you walking in the house, somebody waving at you, you wanting to lose weight, the desire to earn more money, etc. The reminder is the trigger for the reward.

2. Routine is the "action" we believe we have to take in order to experience the reward. If the alarm is the reminder, the routine would be shutting it off. The routine of walking in the house would be shutting the door and locking it. Somebody waving at you would cause you to wave back. The trigger to lose weight may express it's routine in diet change, gaining knowledge, and exercise. The money trigger could cause somebody to work harder, mastermind, gain a new skill set, etc.

3. The reward is the desired outcome or getting your closer to what it is you truly want. The reward for the alarm clock would be waking up on time or eliminating the annoying noise. The reward from shutting the door and locking it is having a safer home. The reward of waving back to somebody is connection. The reward from the prompts of wanting to lose weight or have more money are simply losing weight and having more money!

If there's NO reward, the brain will do everything it can stop it from happening because our mind & bodies are doing everything they possibly can to serve us in the best way it knows based off of our programming. So, we must reward ourselves everytime we do something we don't want to do but know is good for us by changing the association of the outcomes and making sure we do something to acknowledge and reward ourselves for the energy we put out moving towards it.. Even if it's as simple as "great job." Stop feeling like you have to accomplish something huge before you can truly celebrate and appreciate yourself! DO IT NOW! It's **necessary** for your growth.

Reflect

Reflection! To maximize our results and experience, we want to reflect back on what we did right and also where we could've done better - In a constructive way of course, not in a way where we beat ourselves up. Just by taking note of what you did right and could have done better is engraving in the habits of doing the "right" things more & habitually improving yourself. This helps you capitalize on your time, what it is you really want, where you are, and what to get rid of/stop doing.

Shadow Work

Shadow work is the process where you get to learn your "dark" side and bring it to the light. This is the process that we had referenced a ton in this book about removing the blockages dimming your bright, infinite light energy. This is where you discover your limiting beliefs, hidden traumas, insecurities, and so forth. Shadow work is what allows us to transform ourselves. This is where we take any "negativity" & leverage it, grow from it. You do shadow work like this:

1. **Let Natural Contrast Occur**
   Do not go looking to "fix" these things. Remember, fixing is the opposite side of being done. So, the key is remaining aware, conscious that whatever you are irritated by, challenged by, *especially in other people*, is a direct reflection of our shadow. We use emotional intelligence when working with our shadow because anytime we feel less than a high vibrational state of being, we know it's because our emotions are signaling to us that our thoughts are out of alignment in that given moment. Our shadow is the cause for our thoughts being out of alignment. So, step one is being aware of our shadow when it is being active in our life.

2. **Look Within**
Once you realize that the only reason you feel a particular way is because of your shadow, not because of anything going on in the world or what anybody did, you can begin to honestly look within yourself to find out what it is. You identify what the shadow is by targeting what's truly your focus of irritation, your thoughts on it, and what the thought on it means for you. By doing this, you will discover hidden beliefs you were thinking to yourself that were leaking out into your outer reality.

I will give two examples of how someone would work with their shadow. The first is how to stop a shadow from forming and the second is how to deal with a shadow that is already there.

Scenario 1- You get cheated on.

Feelings: angry, upset
Thoughts: How could they do such a thing? Or... Why wasn't I good enough?
Meaning: People can't be trusted... or... There's no point in trying because people are going to do

whatever they want.

Shadow: When I trust people I get hurt... or... No matter how hard I try/good I am, I still won't be enough.

New Choice Of Belief: I choose to now always surround myself with people who acknowledge my worth. I will appreciate a real relationship even more now. I believe the pleasure of love outweighs any temporary pain that may introduce itself along the way. I know this person has their own shadows, they can't feel love if they don't have love for themselves. Therefore, I wish them love and healing as I embrace my own. Not everybody is the same, there are an abundance of trustworthy people here.

***Always go with what feels best!

Scenario 2- Trauma from past relationships

Life Experience: dating new partner, wanting to break up with them
Feeling: irritation, mistrust
Observation of Thoughts: They always have their phone next to them, won't leave the room without it

and is always using it, yet take forever to text me back.
Observation of Meaning: They are clearly hiding something from me. I can't trust them if they are going to be hiding anything from me. Why can't I find somebody who is just as interested as I am?
Observation of Shadow: Trusting intimate partners leaves me vulnerable to get hurt. Or... No matter how hard I try, I'll never be good enough.
Shift In Choice of Beliefs: Vulnerability is my strength, it allows me to be intimate and have a deep connection with others. I choose to acknowledge my worth in every circumstance. This is helping me build trust and allowing privacy with my partner. This is helping me grow deeper with my partner as I address how I truly feel and how we can work together more harmoniously. My partner may have so much going on they don't know how to balance, automate, or leverage things yet. My partner may think they are doing me a favor by not talking to me often as they are either stressed or they believe I want my own space and/or are busy, etc.
Bring It To The Light: So after you have identified what your shadow is, it's time to bring it to the light by parting with it. This can simply be done by asking

yourself: "Do I want to believe this for myself anymore?" If not, then allow yourself to really feel that because remember the more dominant (intense feeling) and consistent (habitual) we think, feel and act in a particular way, the more it becomes apart of who we currently are being. The more it is engraved into our current DNA is the way our programming is set. You already know that if a thought you are thinking is causing you to feel discomfort that it is out of alignment. The more painful the thought, the further out of alignment it is. So, by simply knowing the pain of everything you are putting on the line by not being in alignment with that which you truly want, and aware and feeling all the pleasure that you will have from the change in belief, you can **SHIFT right there and then if you give yourself permission to.** You'll know when you have shifted because you will have experienced what is called "belief breakthrough."

Belief Breakthrough

When you have a true belief breakthrough, you will know it. The exhilarating feeling of getting further into alignment when you have removed a block from your light is unspeakable. To give you an idea of what this feels like in case you're new to this term, you experience a mini version of this when you get into a true psychosomatic state during the proper visualization and affirmation exercises we walked through earlier. That is why you tend you tear up, get goose bumps, have your heart race during those times, or you will just feel "right." Everything about you shifts in a powerful way due to removing just ONE toxic belief. You only want to do belief breakthroughs when needed. Remember: You never want to go digging for what needs "fixed."

To do a belief breakthrough quickly, it's a matter of attaching pain and pleasure to the right areas once you become conscious of the limitation. Remember, our brains are wired to always avoid pain and gaining pleasure. "Pain" and "pleasure" can also be unknown and known subjects because to the subconscious, the unknown is painful. So right now, your subconscious brain thinks it avoids more pain and gains more pleasure living how you currently are based on your current belief system. However, you know by living in the results that that is simply not true. So, to shift how we are subconsciously thinking about this, we will first link all the pain we have been experiencing in our lives from believing that this is true onto the belief whenever it pops up. Whether that be opportunity costs, people you didn't connect with, experiences you could have had, along with what will continuously be withheld if you continue this way. This is one of the few times we will intentionally allow ourselves to feel pain because by allowing ourselves to feel the pain of the belief that has caused it, it really brings to our awareness how it isn't serving us. Then, we want to link pleasure to all the things we want to experience and allow ourselves to really feel it as well. Since one way we find something pleasurable is through what's familiar, the more you practice the good feelings, the more pleasurable it becomes to your subconscious.

Realizing the pain that a belief has caused you is the catalyst to getting you to from a new empowering belief around this subject. You can change your beliefs through the process of using both affirmations and emotional intelligence together and challenging the belief itself. For example, if somebody thought they were ugly, they could either challenge this by saying, " do I really think I'm ugly or am I afraid of other people thinking that?", "how does what I'm insecure about actually help me to my advantage?", "Even if I was ugly, so what? The point of me being beautiful is so that I can experience/have x,y, & z but I can still the fundamentals of those things regardless of how I look so, why am I even worried about that?" & that list goes on. There are many ways to challenge a belief to begin to either reprogram yourself or change the perspective on it. If you are having troubles with how to overcome a particular subject really weighing you down, reach out through the BLIVE community on Facebook or comment on one of my YouTube videos over this.

If you did your belief breakthrough correctly, you will be excited, charged about your new belief and literally feel how you have shifted. Once you have your new belief, you want to ensure that it stays engraved into you by incorporating it into your daily rituals we will soon be speaking about.

An even deeper way of doing belief breakthrough is re-forming the memory around the subject. Our cells build association from our memory of our live experiences. So, anything that triggers that association will enable the cells to act in a way it remembers to know how to. So, when working with my clients, one of the ways I help reprogram them is taking them back to a part in their brain where the memory was originally created for them to create a new association in that memory. Since time is simultaneous and the Law of Rhythm states that everything happens in cycles, seasons, patterns, when we change our memory, we change this "circular timeline" so to speak. This breaks any cycle we have put ourselves on and sets you in a new frequency.

Binaural Beats

Binaural beats are a bio-hack to reprogramming your subconscious brain by using brain frequency technology. How a tool like this works ties in everything you learned about brain waves, how a thought becomes real to the subconscious, and how sound has an influence on our vibration. Binaural beats are structured sounds to vibrate at a particular frequency. Using measured sound frequencies that line up with the way our brain works in theta state, we can bypass the first two layers of the brain much easier. Allowing us to leverage the power of engraving new beliefs from the belief breakthrough and shadow work you've done. Binaural beats also can be used to heal yourself, meditate, get into a particular state of being, and much more. On my YouTube channel you can find both free and exclusive binaural beats to use throughout your journey.

www.youtube.com/elizabethotis

Hypnosis

Hypnosis happens when we get into a particular state of being and our brain waves are operating in theta frequency allowing a "straight pathway" to the subconscious. When in hypnosis, the critical and conscious mind is basically inactive. Remember, everybody is going through hypnotic stages throughout their day, most of us just aren't redirecting it in a leveraged way or intentionally using it in general. Hypnosis is truly one the most leveraged ways you reprogram yourself. Because of this, I specifically use this tool the most to help my clients really make that shift. Being in hypnosis is what feels like a "conscious sleep state." Most people think that if they are hypnotized that they are in a total unaware and trance-like state and that's simply not true...which is why several times throughout the day it is happening without your acknowledgement.

Journaling

Journaling is important in the terms just like silence is but, it creates an even further affirmation since you are writing it out. It allows us to observe what is really going on in our mind/body. Also, when we are "in flow" infinite intelligence begins to speak through writing. Journaling is a great way to process everything that has been going on and also keep your mind sharp on the desires you set intentions for. Writing helps affirm to yourself what you are turning into reality. Some may have heard of "scripting" before using the "55 x 5 method." This is another form of journaling that trains you to really focus on transmuting thought energy into physical because the amount of intention put in through repetition & emotion when doing it. It is also training your neurology on what to be accustomed to.

Set Environment Up For Success

This probably sounds like a "no duh" concept but, it's important to bring this to our awareness because a lot of times a few little tweaks in the way our environment is set up can help us in tremendous ways. Remember, our environment is a huge influence in the way we are thinking & feeling. So, following these 3 things will help set your environment up for exactly what it is you want.

1. **Lift The Vibration Of The Room**
   Intentionally bring things into your environment that help keep your own personal vibration high and that are already of a high vibration such as art, plants, colors, particular scents & minerals, animals. Play binaural beats that have a frequency that aligns with the task you are intending to accomplish. Theta waves aren't the only binaural beat you'll want to turn into. Alpha frequencies will help you get work done in an effective way, there are beats that trigger romantic feeling, etc. Also, remove the things that allow you to feel a low vibration.

2. **Make It Easy To Access**

Begin placing things in plain sight and exactly where you should be interacting with them. For example, put your gym clothes where your feet hit when you first wake up. Keep your journal by your night stand. It's harder to avoid or miss something when it's in plain sight and in the spots where you want to already be interacting with them. Use this in reverse as well. Keep distractions hidden or remove them completely. We also can make things easy access by keeping your important objects in a designated spot.

3. **Correlate To The Vision**

    When we go back to the vision of what we want our end result to look like, how is that environment set up? Part of using the Law of Correspondence & Law of Attraction is to also set up your environment to match what you would be experiencing if you were already living that way. How does the person you want to be treat their environment? How do they have it looking? What are some of the things that person would have in the environment?

What are some things you can do to prepare and "make space" for the things you are manifesting? For example, if you plan on creating a massive business, are you operating from that standpoint through every step you make or are you getting hung up in the "I'm a small business now?" Clearly there are going to be differences in the way you will approach strategies between these two but, we want to make sure we aren't consistently making choices that we will have to undo later just because we weren't keeping that bigger vision in place. Another example is buying a bigger bed or setting your house up to be more "relationship friendly" if you are wanting to be in a happy relationship. If your environment isn't correlating to (a.k.a set up for) what you set intentions for, you're going to induce difficulties on experiencing it.

GDG Sandwich

GDG stands for gratitude, disgust, gratitude. I created this tool you use for whenever you are experiencing something triggering a low emotion, wanting to break a habit, or just are overall going through a tough time. Whenever we begin this process we start by becoming grateful for whatever it is that's causing pain. We can either give thanks by acknowledging the lesson itself in it or just by simply trusting your higher self that it's for your benefit. It's important that we start with gratitude because if we don't make peace with what's bothering us, it's always going to come back no matter how many times we "put the fire out." Start by giving yourself permission to feel gratitude for it. Once you have made peace with it, you want to take note of all of the negative impacts it has had on you and get completely DISGUSTED with the pain it has caused in your life. It seems contradicting but, this creates a standard for yourself. Once you realize how intolerable something really is, you will do no matter what to make sure you stay at least above that certain level.

Think about it, you've definitely had an experience, whether that of been a food, person, scent, where it was so intolerable that it caused you to stay away from experiencing it ever again. It's the same concept here. This causes a shift in your identity towards the person who thrives beyond this circumstance no matter what. The reason we can't start off with disgust is because if we let things drive us from just disgust, not recognizing that it's to evolve us, we tend to actually attract more of it in our lives because we are still fired up about it and also tend to come from a vengeful state. So make peace, celebrate it was for your benefit, then set your standard. Once your standard is set, we can't just leave it there. That's not going to leave you in a high vibration. So, we induce gratitude once more but, this time it's a different kind of gratitude. Instead of gratitude for the situation, now we are giving gratitude for everything that's to come and all of the resources available to you now that you have made this shift. This is reaffirming who you truly are, increasing your overall vibration, & training your mind and body what to be expecting! So simple, yet highly effective.

RECAP!

Now, I know that was a lot to take in. I also know that you want to be as efficient with your time as possible. So don't worry, by the end of this book you will have clarity on how to use these tools in the most efficient way in your life. Now, it's not to say that if you don't do everything on the list, you will not be in alignment. Not the case at all, the fundamental is about becoming a master of your consciousness. These are all just highly effective, scientifically proven tools that aid you in doing so. You want to get in the habit of using the tools you feel urged to use. These are scientific tools that have proven to shape our vibration in the direction we direct it to. Therefore, not just allow us to experience our desires here and there but, also allow us to live a truly fulfilling life. - which is what our true goals are all about. Just like we talked about, many of these tools are already being used throughout the day they just aren't being used in a way that's intentional.

If you are overwhelmed about the amount of things on this list, take a breather! The next chapter will explain how to effectively break this down and also cut additional time off your schedule. So, as we speak of that, let's dive into habitually implementing this into our lives for TRUE transformation!

Chapter 6 – This Is Your Best Friend

Scheduling rituals is a must because since we are forming new habits, we are going to be resistant at times and also forget to actually do it! You may think that's not true because of the impact it's now going to make in your life but, I can assure you, it's going to happen because it's the way we are built. Anytime you interrupt a humans behavior, whether that be adding something new or stopping something, you will be met with resistance. This is your body and mind fighting to stay in what's "safe" (a.k.a familiar). This is something that everybody tends to wrestle with from time to time until it's in automation. Scheduling it in will help ensure you get it done and MAKES sure that it fits with everything else going on in your life.

With that being said, you'll eventually be drawn to doing these activities so much that you are excited to wake up everyday because of what you associate the rituals to. I know you may feel like right now there is not enough time to fit your already schedule in, let alone add self-transformation rituals in, but when using the time freedom log discussed in this book, you'll learn that not only do we have more than enough time in the day when we use leverage and systems but, you have more than enough time in the day when you get clear on what it is you truly want and drop everything else that isn't going to serve you in experiencing that.

The "Time Freedom" Log is in a packet called the "BLIVE Daily Checklist." This checklist was designed to not just remind and help you fit in your conditioning rituals but, to also help you really maximize your time so that you have time freedom as well. Since your life is continuing to change, the "BLIVE Daily Checklist" is available for free download on my website, YouTube Channel, & our BLIVE community group page on Facebook so that you can continue to change and update it.

Now, if we try to change and do everything all at once it throws us into chaos. So, when we are starting to implement these rituals so that they are habitual to us, we want to start by making just a few changes at a time where they matter the most. Those spots are right when we wake up and right before we go to sleep due to the way our brain waves are operating around those times. After working through the hours section in the BLIVE packet, find space to give yourself at least 30 minutes in the morning and night for your rituals.

If you take a look at the chart below, you can see five different brain waves and what the frequency of them look like in each state. The faster the frequency, the more apart we are from high vibrational emotions/experiences, creativity and accessing information from infinite intelligence. This is because the faster the frequency of the thought, the more our brain is using our logical approach, reasoning, which are lower vibrations even though they aren't negative.

When in delta and theta waves, we are in higher vibrations allowing us to access more creative, intuitive thoughts. Also, the thoughts that come to us during these times are easily bypassed by the logical reasoning side of things and allows a more straight path to the subconscious brain. Which is the goal you are looking to accomplish when reprogramming yourself or look within. Think back in reference to how our initial programming was implanted. It's the same when we are operating in theta waves as an adult.

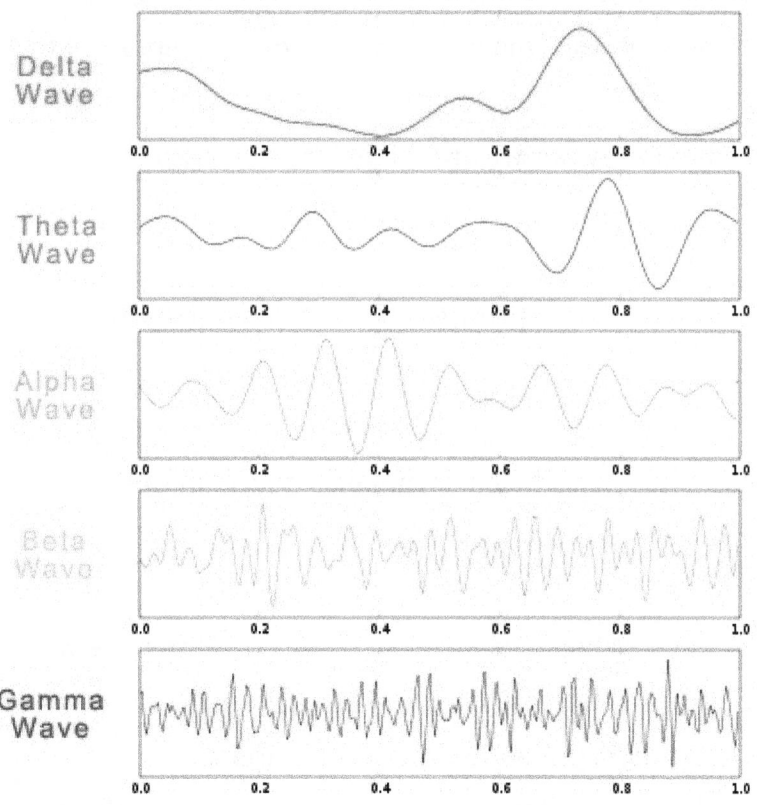

(Side note - high frequency thoughts are not to get mixed with high frequency emotions. They can be opposite in terms of what we are trying to accomplish because a high frequency emotion can still access highly creative/meditative states of being while a high frequency thought is based off of the speed of the brain wave itself and therefore cannot reach states of high creativity and meditation during this time of thought. Gamma waves are the only acceptation to this rule but you do not need to know much about them for what we are talking about here.)

In the first couple hours awakening, due to the way our brain is functioning, the momentum for the day is set off of this. With that being said, we want to intentionally do the things that will really get your mind and body in alignment with the frequency you want when you wake up.

When you wake up, a suggested routine would look like this: Wake up, set intentions, gratitude/prayer, warm water with lemon, silence/meditation/breathwork, visualize, affirm, journal, & some form of physical activity for blood flow. (Eat before and/or after depending on the person).

Things like emotional intelligence, fun, belief breakthrough, and additional nutrition/fluids you would do throughout your day, something you'd stay consistently doing when applicable.

Moving into the night, when we sleep we enter theta and delta waves. This is when using tools like a sleep hypnosis tape, a tool that incorporates both binaural beats & affirmations in it, can be highly leveraged. When we are in the theta brain wave cycle, it is the most suggestible state we can be in. Plus, everybody wishes things were getting done for them while they were sleeping. You can save 1,000x your time now just by working this while you are sleeping not only because you are doing something in your sleep now but, because your programming has roughly 90% of the impact on your results.

 Since there isn't much more we can do while we are sleeping other than something like hypnosis, it's important to take a look at our ritual the hours right before we go to sleep. When we go to sleep our mind is processing everything that has happened through the day, especially everything that happened in the hour and a half right before you go to sleep. The hour and a half right before we go to sleep is very critical in terms of our programming because when we are awake, we have to ability to keep any sort of thought in our critical mind for up to an hour and a half to really analyze if we want it to become a part of our identity or not.

When we go to sleep, our critical mind shuts down and so anything that you were resonating with before then, that you may have shut out if you let your critical mind observe it for the full period of time, gets accepted as a part of you. That can work highly to your advantage or disadvantage which is why I say start with night as well as the morning in developing rituals.

With that being said, setting intentions for tomorrow, visualizing and affirmations are key in this time frame. I also suggest you use a sleep hypnosis with PROPER binary beats to reprogram yourself while you sleep. I made a sleep hypnosis for you because a lot of the ones on YouTube don't have real binary beats nor are the affirmations all properly structured. These are available for free both on my

Youtube & the BLIVE community page.

A couple of other things I would do before I go to sleep is celebrate and reflect. You already know the reasoning for these things and so the reason why we would want to do it at night is because in the morning we want to start with fresh momentum. This is also key in doing before we go to sleep because it anchors in our accomplishments by reprocessing it in our sleep.

Lastly, I would "journal" but journal in a way that affirms who I am/what I am creating & effective correlated game plan for tomorrow. I would plan out the day using the scheduler in the "BLIVE Daily Checklist" and then ask myself the questions listed out to make sure my day tomorrow is planned in correspondence to the frequency of my intended outcomes so that they are achieved. When using this packet properly, you wake up with exact stepping-stones-in-time blocks that help ensure all the things you want to do will flow harmoniously together that day. This packet also has a list of questions included to ensure you are leveraging your time. The "BLIVE Daily Checklist" is ever growing with new tools so, be sure to check back frequently for any new breakthrough tools.

Your body and mind is looking for a "release" at the end of the day to calm down from the days stimulation so, by developing rituals like this at night it will not only help keep you in alignment with what you want but, it will also refrain you from binging out on food, activities or other substances. As I stated earlier, each one of these activities are recommended but, do not get stressed and feel like you have to do every single one. Just make sure you are practicing the fundamentals of all of these tools- which is aligning your dominant energy, expanding your consciousness.

Start by ONLY incorporating 1 or 2 of these habits into your day. I know it seems tempting to go in and change everything but, if you move too fast it will throw your body into chaos. When that happens, it reinforces the belief that the transformation is too hard to make or that you aren't the type of person to stick to your plans and carry them out successfully. It's undeniable that you will face resistance and so we want to minimize the amount of that so that you can go through this process faster and more effectively. It might seem like you'll experience a full transformation quicker by jumping in and doing everything different but, it's actually the opposite. I know it's tempting but trust me on this one, I'm all about going fast & so if it really did make the transformation process faster by changing everything at once I would be saying DO IT. I want to make sure you go as fast as you desire as well so, with that being said, we want to only change up to 2 habits at once. You can begin to add more to the equation whenever you are using the initial chosen tools in automation.

Over time you will find out which tools suit you the best but, now that you know when which tools tend to work the best, you can go back over the list of tools to use and schedule in rituals for both your morning and night. Set your environments up for success wherever you go!

Now, I say this NOT because I don't think you're disciplined, this goes back to the way humans work. I recommend getting an accountability partner so that you are more supported. It doesn't have to be verbal or even with somebody you may know. The reason you want to do this is because as you are shifting out of this reality into the one you set intentions for, not only will you will have natural self imposed resistance but, many of the people around you will be doing things that don't align with this "new you" just because you are in the process of creating a new environment for yourself. Until you been in the process of transition long enough that you change up your environment to correlate to who you are now choosing to be, you will get sick and tired of the environment around you... that is why so many people want to move to a new place when they are going under personal transition.

Think back to the beginning chapter where you learned how your initial programming was formed and how it continuously is formed. A lot of people are realllllllllly comfortable where they are at, regardless of how much they complain, so please do yourself a favor and refresh with somebody who is like-minded with you. This will save you a lot of energy because you are not having to constantly transmute out unwanted energy that can be avoided. The more you put yourself in an environment that serves you, clearly the easier you will thrive. So, make sure you do that for yourself.

If you're like I was when I first started to intentionally shift, I felt like there was nobody personally I could talk about my wild ideas, nobody I knew who thought like me, nobody who was willing to step out of the norm, nobody who was even willing to even really believe, let alone try in what they really wanted for themselves. I felt like I was only surrounded by people who just accepted and settled.

Yet, I knew there were people out there in the world but, I just didn't personally know them yet and didn't yet have an idea of where to meet and connect with them. So, to stay sane with my human need for connection and to be "alike" (remember we all have this need) I choose to connect to people I looked up to with my imagination. Some of the people I admire are: Grant Cardone, Tony Robbins, Mary Kay Ash. These were the people I saw my "true" self being around and acting like. So, what I would do to stay accountable with them is I would always ask myself, "what would I be doing if they were here right now?" When I would be frustrated and in need of guidance, I would quiet my mind (get in theta brain waves), and ask myself the questions I would ask them and just listen for their response. Just like how you are tuning into the frequency of that which you want to experience, you can do the same to receive messages from other beings - even if you dont know them personally.

You know now that you have an arsenal full of weapons & tools in order face trying times and experiencing what it is you want. However, it is important to bring this next chapter to you from a place of additional awareness, perseverance, and community so that you keep thriving in your journey.

Chapter 7 – Logically, It Doesn't Make Much Sense

As we approach the end of this book, I would like to say that I have no doubt in you whatsoever that you will obtain what your heart and soul set intentions for. As I just wrapped up in the last chapter though, we both know that there will continue to be trying times. Times that will challenge you, make you feel like you did a bunch of work for nothing, make you feel like you aren't cut out for it, you may have already experienced some of these times. Just because you have all these tools on your side and your faith may be stronger than ever right now doesn't mean that the storms won't still come of course. Contrast is part of the process baby! It shows us exactly what we want and births new ideas to create. I say this only with encouragement, to remind you that sometimes you could be doing everything right, and things still come crashing down on you. It's just a part of the process, to show us more of what we want and guide us in that direction. Keep your faith high and keep preserving, storms are temporary and EVERYTHING is for a reason. When "bad" things are happening it could be because we need to tune our vibration to get back into frequency or that we simply are just viewing it from a "bad" lense, which is also being out of alignment with the frequency you want. Don't beat yourself up when starting to face resistance. This goes to show you are making progress... eat a GDG Sandwich if you need to.

Remember, our ENTIRE reality is based upon what frequency our personal vibration is resonating at. Whatever frequency we are on determines what we see, hear, smell, taste, touch, think, feel, and action we take. It is those things that then determine how we receive and perceive the current reality as we know in this moment. So, whenever you feel out of alignment, the VERY first thing you MUST DO in order to succeed is get back into alignment by using your emotional intelligence to redirect your thoughts in a way that serves you.

As we mentioned throughout this book, The

Law of Duality states that everything in this universe has two equal, opposite energies that come together in order for it to come into creation. Dark has Light. Hot has cold. This means the same stick of our best life, is the same stick as our worst life. Sometimes in the turmoil, sometimes in the transformation process, the negative sides are experienced because of our shadow. The negatives are there to see which side of the stick you really want to be on. The negatives are there to really guide you into a direction where you are best served at. When we work with our shadow and use the tools gained from this book, we inevitably move up the ladder and into the vibrational frequency of that which we desire.

Remember, the Law of Correspondence states that nothing in this universe happens for no reason. So, if something rough is going on, it just goes to show what you are giving off vibrationally and how you either need to shift the direction of doing things or thinking.

As you know from earlier chapters, The Law of Gestation is also a thing. So, sometimes our intended manifestations take their bittersweet time. This is just something to get more excited about because we will appreciate it more when it comes. It's important to remind yourself of this because it helps keep our vibration consistent in order to stay on track. However, this is not something to get too caught up in because things can happen a lot quicker than you think sometimes. Remember, time isn't real. Always be willing to be in it as long as it takes, but believe it doesn't have to take any time at all. Believe that just because most people coming from "linear time" that lived and viewed a particular situation to be "just the way it is" or "just the way it works" doesn't mean that it has to be that way. You don't operate in linear time anymore. You know what time really is now. View "miracles" as normal and that's what they become.

    Another thing to take note of and to be encouraged by is the combination of The Law of Oneness and The Law of Perpetual Transmutation of Energy. Together these laws help us stay encouraged and excited about what's to come.Together they basically yield that whatever you desire and are working towards HAS to come into fruition. When we have a solid strategy in place & are working towards it like crazy yet not seeing results, it can be extremely frustrating. Nothing to fuss about however, these two laws got your back! When we have a strategy supposed to yield particular results, we expect those results to come in that particular way. However the universe doesn't always work like that. Remember the universe, infinite intelligence, knows best. So, if you are not getting the result you want after putting in the work, the universe will either bring you what you want (or better) through another avenue OR it will bring you a teacher, message, tools of some sort to show you how to get into alignment so that you can obtain it. That might have been what happened with you reading this book. Chances are, you are reading this book because you had gotten to a point where you were burnt out in life. If that's you, reading this book right now, this book was a gift from the universe to you. Elizabeth doesn't even type when this book is being written. Infinite intelligence does. Know that the universe wants you to flourish in your pure desires and you are worthy beyond all measure as it is what you came here to do.

When you are going through any sort of

transformation, there's of course the sexy and the ugly. There's the pain and there's the pleasure. There's the enemies and there's your fellow warriors. To B-LIVE is Being-LIVE. BLIVE is culture, way of living but, it is also a community. A place and family of individuals just like you. Who feel just like you, who walked through rocky paths just like you, who have on soul purposed desires and dream big JUST LIKE YOU. I encourage you to plug into the movement & become a part of the family. Let yourself be surrounded and supported by unconditional loving spirits who want to help support you and see you shine, just as much as your highest self would.

This journey can be crazy and challenging at times, it is also filled with exhilarating, breathtaking, timeless moments where everything seems to be working in harmony. Together we stand by our fellow BLIVERS and lift each other up, support each other in our goals and endeavors. Below I have listed a link to join the community once again for you to get plugged into the movement. BLIVERS are all over the world and soon to be having event centers near you. To stay connected through any time however, we use this group. In this group I give free weekly teachings further on these subjects, daily juice for inspiration and education, and updates about where we are going as a movement! Grab a friend and we will be ready to welcome you guys as fellow BLIVERS.

www.facebook.com/groups/blivemovement

Chapter 8-
Imagine A World Where

Imagine a world where everybody lived for their purpose. A world where everybody embraced the pure, limitless creator they truly are. Where everybody believed in infinite possibilities and harmoniously co-created with the universe? Can you imagine what kind of world that would be like? There would be no environmental damage, there would be no disease causing harm, there would be no suicides, there would be no war, there would be no conditional love, there would be no constant frustration in the day to day life. People would be happy, living in their purpose. Nobody would have shortage consciousness and be living in lack. Can you imagine a world like that?

Well, here the thing, the world CAN be like that. We just need to all do our part by raising our personal vibration, being an example, and helping educate and lead others who are unaware. End the control, the limitations, the brainwash. This world is literally limitless and we have access to all of it's power. Let's all begin to step into that life as a collective.

This book has been jam packed with information, tools, & techniques to help you identify your life's purpose, set limitless, authentic intentions around them & how to literally reprogram, condition your body and mind to be in alignment with those things so that you can experience them. As stated earlier however, this book does no good with just being information in your head. Yes, you have now a tangible packet to work off of to help implement habits into your life. However, let's ENSURE this transformation continues to take place. Not just get it started but, to actually keep the momentum going & rolling, allowing you to live a completely fulfilled life where you are Being-LIVE. Experiencing all that you desire, impacting the world on a positive level. The best way to do that is staying accountable by spreading this information & helping others do the same with their lives. Plus, what fun is it to experience a life in flow all by yourself? Don't you want people to join you in their own joy ride as well? Isn't there people you know that are wasting time and energy, completely unhappy each day of their lives?

You and I both know that it is part of our duty to spread this information to the people who need it. You and I both know the planet needs us as a collective to do our part. Look at all the people and LIFE itself suffering due to the ignorance of this topic! So, I have three accountability challenges for you to complete to help you both keep yourself in alignment & help others to do the same. Out of every 500 people who do these things, I will randomly draw an individual to have a 1 on 1 hour session with me. You will have the opportunity to use this session to ask me any questions you may have but, whatever the session entails has the same outcome no matter what- that is allowing you to shift into alignment with what it is your truly desire and expand your consciousness. So, with that being said, we may practice hypnotherapy, do an in depth belief breakthrough, and for fourth. Since this individual is randomly drawn, the session will be tailored to better serve this individual.

The reason why I am willing to give away this time for free is because the ultimate goal is to help cause legendary breakthroughs in the way that the world thinks, observes, and behaves. Helping restore the light back to each individual on this planet, therefore mother nature herself as well. Restoring life back into the planet by also embracing our own. Helping create a world where everybody is able to seek solutions to their problems simply, live out their purpose, be absolutely creative and design amazing arts, technologies. A world where we learned how to fully embrace our personal power so we could live out our limitless desires and breakthrough collectively. Where we would then even know how to do next level consciousness stuff like shapeshift & walk through walls. It's all possible, we just have to first be in the frequency to find out how or what to do! You learned how to match the frequency of anything by reading this book. You will go on to be one of the people who invents, discovers, or teaches the world some of these "crazy" things and causes that legendary breakthrough. With that being said, here are the 3 challenges:

CHALLENGE #1: Take a picture of yourself holding

this book and post it to your social media pages. Tag 3 friends teaching them something powerful you learned from this book that could also help them. Tag me in it as well! My social media name is "Elizabeth Otis" on all social media platforms... Except Instagram, which is: @elizabeth_otis333. Use the hashtag **#ReinventYourself**

CHALLENGE #2: Post a review under where you bought this book at! Reviews help the algorithm suggest the book to more people, causing a bigger impact. Take a picture for proof.

CHALLENGE #3: Join & invite 50+ people to the BLIVE community group on Facebook with a brief message letting them know why you think they would be good in this group. The message can be the same for each person as long as it applies to them. I'm able to know when somebody invites another person to our community, so you don't have to worry about it tracking anything other than making sure you get to 50!

These challenges are designed to help hold you accountable in the education you learned, be plugged into our community for further transformation and questions, and do your part in helping spread light on this planet. All of these challenges are made to benefit you & as a bonus for doing it, you have the chance to be awarded with a priceless 1-on-1 transformation session. I can't wait to get to know more about you, your goals and missions. I am looking forward to hearing from you soon.

Chapter 9 – You Are Legendary

As we end this book, the most important thing for me to say to you is thank you. Thank you for not just taking the time to educate yourself on this topic but, thank you for not giving up.

Thank you for continuing to fight and persevere. I know you have been through hell. I know you have been through the floods. You wouldn't have resonated with this book if otherwise. I know it hasn't been easy for you the majority of the time. You are limitless energy though. You are somebody who does not give up despite all the times you wanted to. You are somebody who is coming back for their victories and to experience all that you came here for, you are somebody who is going to leave a huge imprint on the world with the presence you bring to it through your gifts, skills, and true personality. Thank you so much for fighting for a better way for yourself, not settling any longer. Your presence is so important here on planet earth and we need you to fulfill your missions so that we can all thrive as a whole.

    Thank you for fighting for us & going after your dreams. You deserve every blessing on the way to you. You deserve every exhilaration on the way to you. You are so worthy and appreciated for simply being and embracing all that you truly are. So thank you my friend, I know this road has not been easy but, you are on the same road that shares paradise. Forever on now, you will never be the same.

You are a BLIVER.

& as always, Dream Big, Live Large, #BLIVE

INDEX

Chopra, Deepak. *Quantum Healing: Exploring the Frontiers of Mind/Body Medicine.* 1989. (Excerpt from pg. 134)

Grafton, Scott. *Physical Intelligence: The Science of how the Body and the Mind Guide Each Other.* 2020 (Excerpt taken from pg. 6)

Pg. 51 – Vibration Chart. Image courtesy of: https://thriveglobal.com/stories/how-to-become-the-best-version-of-yourself-by-raising-your-vibration/

Pg. 38 – Brain waves chart. Image courtesy of: https://itsusync.com/different-types-of-brain-waves-delta-theta-alpha-beta-gamma-ezp-9

About the Author

Elizabeth Otis is a high-energy, transformation NUT. She is a best selling author, hypnotherapist, and the CEO & Founder of the BLIVE movement. The movement was created to teach people how to break free of limitations, consciously create one's own reality, identify what they came to planet Earth for and have a space for people to thrive in. She focuses on helping people achieve their desires through science, how to be fulfilled through living in their true identity, and how to be one with their consciousness. Her goal is to help people elevate, flourish and understand their spiritual journey through science. There are multiple ways to learn more about Elizabeth: you can watch her video teachings on her YouTube channel; connect through the BLIVE movement, the books she has written, or her self-transformation products and services.

"My commitment to helping people design a life that truly serves them & breaks them free of limitation is what keeps the fire burning underneath me & charge to my life. I understand what it's like to have strong,

massive, desires, & to feel like you're doing everything you possibly can to get it yet, still not experience it. After learning the sciences that predominantly affect the way we experience our reality & obtain anything in the world, my life forever changed. My mission is to take the BLIVE culture, knowing how to consciously create one's own reality, and get that information over to a minimum of 7 billion people. The mission of this is so that each individual can live out their lives' purpose and we as a planet are enlightened."

Connect Further with Elizabeth & Join the BLIVE Movement

www.youtube.com/elizabethotis

www.facebook.com/groups/blivemovement

Blive checklist is available inside the BLIVE community & in YouTube descriptions

www.ingramcontent.com/pod-product-compliance
Lightning Source LLC
Chambersburg PA
CBHW071440160426
43195CB00013B/1974